Pathfinder Pilot

The Wartime Memoirs of Wing Commander R.A. Wellington DSO, OBE, DFC

Pen & Sword

AVIATION

First published in Great Britain in 2020 by
Pen & Sword Aviation
An imprint of
Pen & Sword Books Ltd
Yorkshire – Philadelphia

ISBN 978 1 52677 970 0

A CIP catalogue record for this book is
available from the British Library.

Printed and bound in the UK by TJ International Ltd, Padstow, Cornwall.

Pen & Sword Books Limited incorporates the imprints of Atlas, Archaeology,
Aviation, Discovery, Family History, Fiction, History, Maritime, Military, Military
Classics, Politics, Select, Transport, True Crime, Air World, Frontline Publishing,
Leo Cooper, Remember When, Seaforth Publishing, The Praetorian Press,
Wharncliffe Local History, Wharncliffe Transport, Wharncliffe True Crime and
White Owl.

For a complete list of Pen & Sword titles please contact

PEN & SWORD BOOKS LIMITED
47 Church Street, Barnsley, South Yorkshire, S70 2AS, England
E-mail: enquiries@pen-and-sword.co.uk
Website: www.pen-and-sword.co.uk

Or
PEN AND SWORD BOOKS
1950 Lawrence Rd, Havertown, PA 19083, USA
E-mail: Uspen-and-sword@casematepublishers.com
Website: www.penandswordbooks.com

Contents

Foreword

As the number of ex-Bomber Command airmen has dwindled in the last decade, so have the memoirs being published of their experiences. Now that the last of the surviving airmen are well into their nineties, it's pleasing to find this new account coming to light.

The pull of the RAF to young men from the Commonwealth and other countries around the world was strong, and in P/O Wellington's case this was no exception. Although British by birth, the young Wellington was living and working in Brazil as a farmer when war broke out, and even after a disastrous initial foray into flying that would have put most people off forever, he stuck with it and qualified as a Bomber Pilot in early 1942.

Wimpy arrived at 106 Squadron soon after Guy Gibson had taken over in April 1942 and flew under his command for most of the time that he was the Squadron Commander. Although not part of Gibson's 'inner circle' of officers, and admitting that he 'never hit it off very well with Gibson as a person', he still had the highest admiration for him as leader, and indeed the respect was mutual; in *Enemy Coast Ahead* Gibson describes Wimpy as 'one of the great men of 106 Squadron'. He was awarded both the DFC and DSO during his time there and flew thirty-four ops.

After completing his tour, Wimpy went straight on to join 83 Squadron Pathfinders and a few months later renewed his acquaintance with Squadron Leader John Searby, who had made the same transition from 106 Squadron to become Squadron Commander at RAF Wyton. After successfully completing a further twenty-six ops, he had to stand down from operational flying for medical reasons.

Wimpy then transferred to No.8 (Pathfinder Force) Group headquarters in Huntingdon and there continued his involvement with Bomber Command, working closely under its commander, Air Commodore Don Bennett.

Because of these connections alone, Wimpy's memoir gives a great insight into the Allied bombing campaign; but it goes on to give a further fascinating account of post-war Brazil, to which he returned and where he had an outstanding career as Consul, a role in which he was awarded the OBE for his services.

Although Wimpy attempted to have this memoir published when he was alive, it has fallen to his daughter Sandra to give it the recognition it deserves. It will be a great addition to the squadron records of both 106 and 83 Squadrons and the lesser known workings of Pathfinder Group Headquarters.

Clive Smith
106 Squadron researcher and author

Acknowledgements

My very special thanks to Clive Smith (clivesmith@106squadron.com) and Charles Foster, both of whom I met over the internet when I noticed they were researching my father's wartime career. Clive Smith is the author of *Lancaster Bale Out* (published by Mention the War, 2018), which he wrote as a result of his research into his second cousin Sergeant Jack Hougham (shot down on 8 July 1943 over Cologne), who flew with 106 Squadron at RAF Syerston with a bomb aimer called Fred Smooker, who survived the war. Clive Smith eventually tracked down and interviewed Fred Smooker and wrote his account of his RAF wartime experiences. Charles Foster is the nephew of the Dams Raid pilot, Squadron Leader David Maltby DSO, DFC, who was killed on 14/15 September 1943 when his aircraft and crew went down in the North Sea after an aborted mission to bomb the Dortmund Ems Canal. Charles Foster is the author of *Breaking the Dams* (Pen & Sword, 2008) and *The Complete Dambusters* (The History Press, 2018), and also runs the dambuster blog (dambustersblog.com).

Their combined specialist knowledge and advice relating to Bomber Command have proved invaluable. Both kindly revised the original text and made some very pertinent suggestions and additions (including providing the official dates of the deaths of fellow crew members and identifying Bomber Command photographs), which have been incorporated into my father's original text to give further emphasis to points raised by the author. Clive Smith also kindly agreed to write the foreword to *Pathfinder Pilot*. I am indebted to them both.

My many thanks to my cousin, Christina Wellesley-Smith (née Pretyman) for kindly providing a photograph of herself with her father, Walter Pretyman and Air Marshal Sir Arthur Harris, Commander-in-Chief of RAF Bomber Command.

My thanks also go to an old family friend, the author, artist and garden designer, Laurence Fleming, who we first met in Brazil when he was studying with the famous Brazilian landscape gardener, Roberto Burle Marx. His close and long-term friendship with my parents and his enthusiasm for my father's work have made him a most valuable ally, especially with regard to writing the preface.

Last but by no means least, I would like to thank Major Niall Hall MVO, Regimental Adjutant, Irish Guards, who kindly put me in touch with Henry Wilson at Pen & Sword, who made this publication possible.

All of these enthusiastic and esteemed colleagues make me feel confident that the final layout, choice of illustrations and other pertinent information do justice to my father's wartime memories and would therefore meet with his full approval.

Sandra I. Wellington

Preface

Richard Anthony Wellington, always known as 'Tony', was born in Moseley, Birmingham, England on 6 July 1919. His parents were Alec M. Wellington, then the Superintendent of the São Paulo Railway in Brazil, and Dorothy (née Marshall). Tony was the only nephew of the late Lieutenant Colonel Neville Marshall VC, MC, Irish Guards/Lancashire Fusiliers.

Tony was taken by his parents to Brazil shortly after his birth. In 1926 he was sent back to England to be educated at Bigshotte boarding school in Wokingham, Berkshire with his elder brother Jack, who died there in 1929 as the result of an inadequately treated injury in a skating accident. Tony went on to study at Newlands House, Harrow School (1933–6) before returning to Brazil to farm at the family property located near the town of Atibaia, in the state of São Paulo.

In November 1940 Tony returned to England and volunteered for the RAF, soon earning himself the nickname 'Wimpy'. After extensive training, he was commissioned as a Pilot Officer and in March 1942 joined 106 Squadron at RAF Coningsby under the command of Wing Commander Guy Gibson to begin operational flying. In February 1943, after thirty-four sorties, he and his crew joined 83 Pathfinder Squadron at RAF Wyton airbase. At this stage of the war, the average life expectancy of Bomber Command crew was around three weeks.

In March 1943, Tony was awarded a DFC. The citation read as follows:

F/O R.A. Wellington has participated in many operational sorties, a large number of which have been against targets in the Ruhr. He has defied the heaviest opposition to bomb his objectives, and on several occasions his aircraft has been damaged. One night in July 1942, whilst over Wilhelmshaven, his aircraft was heavily engaged by anti-aircraft fire, and later was attacked by an enemy fighter. The bomber sustained severe damage, but F/O Wellington skillfully flew it back to base.

In July 1943, he was awarded a DSO, the citation reading as follows:

Acting Squadron Leader R. A. Wellington DFC (106238), RAFVR, No. 83 Squadron. This officer has completed a large number of sorties, including eighteen attacks on the Ruhr area. His efforts throughout have been characterized by a keen desire to bomb his targets determinedly and accurately. Squadron Leader Wellington is a fine leader whose great skill and example have contributed to the high morale of the air crews of the squadron.

During his wartime service, Tony completed a total of two tours, or sixty sorties, involving mainly night-time bombing raids over Germany, Italy, France, Czechoslovakia and the North Sea. His attitude to life was very much in accordance with the unofficial Pathfinder motto, to 'press on regardless', and throughout his life he always spoke of his belief in 'walking that extra mile'.

In June 1943, Tony was declared medically unfit to continue flying due to a serious ear injury and was detailed to serve as a PFF staff officer. In December 1943, he was sent on an official RAF lecture tour of Brazil to promote the Allied cause. He travelled via New York, where he met with Randolph Hearst, who asked him to write about his wartime experiences for *Cosmopolitan* magazine. At the end of his Brazilian lecture tour, in February 1944, he married Irene Smallbones, daughter of the British Consul General, at St Paul's Church in São Paulo. They eventually had six children, four of whom died shortly after birth. Their surviving son was born in 1945, and their daughter in 1948. On his return to Britain, Tony was promoted to Wing Commander and in August 1944 was appointed Air Attaché at the British Embassy in Lisbon, where he served until April 1946. Before returning to England, he was responsible for organizing a friendly football match between the official RAF team (including Stanley Matthews) and the Portuguese Army team. After his demobilization in September of that year, he returned to Brazil as representative of the De Havilland Aircraft Company for Latin America. On termination of his contract in 1948, he and his family went back to farm at Atibaia.

In 1951, Tony and Irene decided to return to England. Tony joined the Diplomatic Service but, in 1953, after his first overseas posting to Germany, he resigned to work as ships' manager for the South Coast Sand & Ballast Company in Southampton. When this was sold off after the Suez Crisis in 1956, Tony rejoined the Diplomatic Service, serving in London, again in Germany, in Iran and in Spain. In 1963, he was appointed H.M. Consul at Recife, with a district covering nine states in the north and north-east of Brazil. He and Irene actively supported the local British community, and Tony was involved in organizing many different events, including a pioneering 'ecumenical service', held at the Anglican Church, which had as one of its speakers Dom Helder Câmara, the Catholic Archbishop of Recife and Olinda. During this posting, he was made an honorary member of the local Foundation for Space Activities and Studies.

In 1965, Tony was transferred to H.M. Embassy at Rio de Janeiro as Press Information Officer and on two occasions served as temporary head of the British Embassy in the new capital of Brasilia. He was a member of the UK observer delegation to the OAS Conference in Rio de Janeiro (1965) and leader of the UK delegation to the Conference of Plenipotentiaries for the Conservation of Atlantic Tuna held at Rio de Janeiro in 1966. In 1969, he was awarded the Order of Rio Branco by the Brazilian government.

Tony was a great supporter of Polish ex-servicemen in Rio de Janeiro and, as a result, they made him an honorary member of the Polish ex-Combatants' Association and awarded him their Gold Emblem and medal, as well as a symbolic payment (in Polish currency) of his first 'salary' as a serving officer.

He was awarded an OBE in 1972 and retired from the diplomatic service in 1973, later joining British Caledonian Airways as public relations officer for Brazil. He also worked for the *Jornal do Brasil* and for more than eight years wrote regular articles about Brazil for the *Money Manager*, a New York financial weekly. Due to his keen interest in and long-term knowledge of the country, Tony was commissioned to write a book entitled *The Brazilians – How they live and work*, published by David & Charles in 1974. In 1975, he resigned from the *Jornal do Brasil* and moved to Natal,

Rio Grande do Norte, to work for Companhia Algimar, which he did for a while, before returning to Rio.

Even during the long periods spent living abroad, he always remained an active member of the Pathfinder Association in London and kept in regular touch with several members of his wartime crew.

As a person, Tony was always discreet and had a wonderful wry sense of humour. Typical of his generation, he rarely discussed his private emotions and preferred to use an amusing observation or anecdote to help overcome any difficult situation. In spite of having lived for so many years in Brazil, a close friend and colleague described him as remaining 'totally and uncompromisingly English', and he always maintained a keen sense of patriotic duty to 'King and Country'.

Wherever they lived, Tony and his wife enjoyed a wide circle of friends, including local writers, artists, musicians, politicians, military personnel and businessmen, as well as other members of the diplomatic corps. Tony was also an excellent horseman and a two-goal handicap polo player. In 1957, he played for the winning English team – captained by Jimmy Edwards – at Phoenix Park in Dublin. He was also a keen follower of the Turf and even bred his own racehorse, rather predictably named 'Waterloo'.

Tony spoke Portuguese, Spanish and German fluently. He played the Spanish guitar and used to entertain friends with his fine voice, singing mainly sea shanties, calypsos, English and Brazilian folk songs and wartime ballads, as well as playing Spanish flamencos. In conjunction with a Spanish colleague, he produced a series of instructional records/booklets for aspiring guitarists.

He was a keen and talented photographer and also held a long interest in Brazilian Indians. On several occasions, he visited the Kadiweu tribe at their reservation at Bodoquena in Southern Mato Grosso and documented many of their traditional face and body paintings. At the request of their captain – or chief – he later wrote a book about the tribe entitled *The Horsemen Indians of Brazil*. He also visited the Karaja Indians on the Island of Bananal, the Tiriyo in Amazonas and the Kaiapo in Mato Grosso, and organized a special visit by the then British Ambassador, Sir David Hunt, and Lady Hunt, to the Xavante and Bororo groups, also in the Mato Grosso. In 1968, Tony helped form a small expedition, accompanied by

Rikpaktsa Indian guides, that made an attempt to contact the famous tribe of 'Amazon women', then said to be living in the isolated depths of the Mato Grosso forest. It was during this same trip that Tony discovered the whereabouts of Colonel Percy Fawcett's gold signet ring, given to one of his guides during his last fateful journey and which was eventually returned to the Fawcett family in England. Tony went on to write several books and articles on the history of Brazil; he also gave radio talks on the BBC and was a Fellow of the Royal Geographical Society.

After retiring from the Foreign Office, Tony and Irene decided to remain in Brazil, since they believed the warm climate would be more beneficial to their health (both suffered from emphysema). After living in various locations, they eventually settled in Petropolis, in the State of Rio de Janeiro.

Following a long illness and after spending nearly five months in intensive care, Tony died on 7 April 1992 at the São Silvestre Hospital in Rio de Janeiro at the age of seventy-two. In recognition of his distinguished wartime service, the Royal British Legion requested that Tony Wellington be buried with full honours in their section of the British Cemetery at Gamboa, Rio de Janeiro. One of his pallbearers was Yunaki, a young Yawalapiti Indian. One year later, the Yawalapiti tribe in the Xingu honoured Tony with a special *Kuarup* festival, held in memory of dead chiefs.

Chapter 1

Farming in Brazil

The outbreak of the Second World War in September 1939 found me farming rather unsuccessfully in Brazil. In the long run, it might perhaps have been better if I had followed up an enthusiastic urge to apply for a short service commission in the Royal Air Force which came over me during my time at school in England. I even went so far as to buy a book full of photographs showing fascinating RAF aeroplanes, and the thought of actually flying them was really exciting. The RAF appealed to me as a dashing sort of service, but my notions of what one did in it were largely influenced by a film called 'The Camels are Coming', in which Jack Hulbert, wearing that attractive uniform, flew out single-handed from romantic Beau Geste forts in the desert and demolished fearful odds before returning safely to base. For me his performance exercised much more of a magnetic recruiting influence than the rather bullying 'Your Country Needs You' type of poster. Why should other adventurous spirits not join the RAF and emulate Jack Hulbert? Clearly, the first thing to do was to get up in an aeroplane and see what the air felt like.

The experiment was disastrous. Having finally given way to my pleadings, an aerial photographer friend took me up in the early 1930s for twenty terrifying minutes in his rattle-trap Gipsy Moth. We took off from Gatwick, then a grass airfield, and the pilot's shouts, which I could not hear properly, and gesticulations, which I did not understand, merely confirmed my worst fears that Nemesis was about to overtake us. Apparently, the flight was quite normal, but I shall never forget it. The glamour of flying went overboard during those awful twenty minutes, and I returned thankfully to earth with the firm conviction that farming was the life for me.

Farming was fun, but a combination of poor land and no capital made it unprofitable. Nevertheless, I spent three very enjoyable years running our property near the town of Atibaia in the State of São Paulo, Brazil, where the climate was perfect and the friendliness of the countryside and its inhabitants a delight to live with. The farm was about fifty miles from São Paulo, and in those days of the late 1930s the journey by car took about two hours over a gravel road with plenty of dust or mud on the way, according to the latest weather. Atibaia is at an altitude of 3,000ft and enjoys such a good climate that the original Brazilian Indian inhabitants called it 'the healthy place'. There was bright sunshine during most days of the year, and the nights were so cold that I was glad of a log fire in the sitting room. The farm covered 720 acres, stretching from the top of a rocky hill at the back of the house over rolling pastures down to the River Atibaia in the valley. Its main crop had always been hill coffee which, though more difficult to work because of the terrain, earned a better price for its special flavour. There could be no mechanization on the steep hillside, and when the crop was harvested it had to be brought down to the washing tank and drying yard in great baskets on the backs of mules. Coffee had been the farm's income for years, but at the time I went to live there the price had dropped to rock bottom, with the result that much of Brazil's main product was being dumped in the sea or burned in railway locomotives, because there was no market for it. With the price as it was we could no longer afford the wages to keep up the coffee plantation, and I therefore had no alternative but to cut down the trees and create pasture in their place for running beef cattle.

The first herd I bought consisted of sixty innocent-looking Zebu or Brahman cattle, with characteristic humps, long ears and liquid eyes. They had to be collected from a town about fifty miles away, where they had recently arrived from their native state of Mato Grosso. Two of my men and I went there with our horses in order to drive the cattle through the town and entrain them for the journey in cattle trucks to our local railway station, about three miles away from the farm. These Zebu cattle can be very fierce individually but as a herd they will usually follow a rider in front of them while two other horsemen keep them together from the back and sides. On our way to the railhead all went well until we were in the middle of the town, when something suddenly upset the cattle and, in spite of our efforts, they stampeded in all directions. Chaos resulted. The scene was something like the running of the bulls in Pamplona, although in this case the local citizens were not trying to display their courage but merely to escape the charges of the angry Zebu, which had obviously been nursing a hitherto hidden grievance against the human race. A schoolteacher escaped with her life by inches, while a man faced at a yard's range with a two-horned antagonist preparing to deliver the *coup de grâce* managed to divert its attention for a moment by throwing his hat on the ground and then got to safety on what appeared to be winged feet. Survival was to the swiftest, and there must have been more speed records broken that day than at any Olympics. Luckily, no one was injured, and we finally managed to get the herd together again and back to the corral we had started from. Next day, we succeeded in driving the cattle to the railhead without incident, but as we went through the town there was not a soul in sight, and all the houses and shops were understandably shuttered and barred.

Our troubles were not over by half, although the Zebu were as good as gold during the train journey. We arrived back at our small railway station at about 9.00 pm, and since it was getting dark, I told the stationmaster we would leave the cattle in the trucks overnight and pick them up the next morning. I had just climbed on to my horse when there was a rending crash as the Zebu started to break open the cattle trucks, which were made of really thick wooden bars. In front of our astonished eyes, those cattle came pouring out through the mangled debris and without hesitation jumped over a five-barred gate out of the yard in a style which would have been the envy of any Grand National horse. The last one disappeared into the darkness; there were now sixty head of cattle roaming the countryside. I thought desperately of the damage they could do to my neighbours' crops and, even worse, to any people wandering abroad who might have the misfortune to cross their path. Luckily, the moon came up, and by its light we were able to follow the course of devastation until we finally caught up with our wandering Zebu. It took us three hours to round them up and get them safely into a large pasture we had prepared for them at the farm, with stout fence posts and five strands of barbed wire around it. Thankfully, I went to bed after what had been an eventful two days, secure in the knowledge that our troubles were over. Early next morning, an irate citizen telephoned me from Atibaia, nearly three miles away, to complain that my cattle were now roaming the town at will and frightening the daylights out of the local populace. The whole thing was becoming a nightmare, and the ownership of these cattle something of an embarrassment. We rounded them up once again and drove them back into their pasture, but none of us had any confidence that they would stay there. Strangely enough, they never broke out or strayed again from that moment on, although probably no amount of barriers could have stopped them had they wanted to go elsewhere. Clearly, they had now accepted the field as home.

Life on the farm was not usually as hectic as this, however, and the days generally provided a pleasant routine of work until the time came in the evening to light the Aladdin paraffin lamps and read a book or play the gramophone before going to bed at an early hour. When living by myself got too lonely, I went to the small cinema in Atibaia, especially if the Lone Ranger series was being shown, and called in at the quite good hotel there for a meal and a chat with the nice couple who ran it. My transport consisted of a 1928 Chevrolet pick-up lorry bought from the local garage owner. Drivers of lorries had to hold professional driving licences, but in my case there was no problem about obtaining one because the man I bought the lorry from was the official examiner for such licences. Since it was a case of 'no licence, no sale', I rather understandably passed the far from arduous test with flying colours. The only bore about it was that professional drivers had to wear a chauffeur's cap, and this created an amusing spectacle when I took a girlfriend to the theatre in São Paulo and arrived there wearing white tie and tails and that wretched cap.

On the farm, or *fazenda*, we employed a number of men for cattle work, milking and planting; together with their families, they totalled about seventy souls. Each family occupied one of the farm cottages, simple brick and tile buildings with beaten earth floors, and had a small plot of land on which to grow maize and vegetables. Every man worked on a daily wage basis and earned the equivalent of about £1 sterling (then nearly US$5) a month. I thought this very little even for those days and increased the rate quite considerably. The result was that all my men worked fewer days in the month to earn exactly the same monthly wage they had earned before the increase. Obviously, they knew how to live on that sum and were not a bit interested in getting more. In many cases, their vitality was sapped by intestinal worms, but it was quite impossible to persuade them to see a doctor or take any medicine. They would go to the local *curandeiro* or healer in case of serious illness, which they usually believed was caused by an enemy putting the evil eye on them through *macumba* or voodoo. It was a long time before I discovered with surprise that my headman Benedito was the High Priest of voodoo in the locality and that he presided over strange rites and ceremonies in a cave on the hill at the back of the farm. I was never invited to these gatherings, nor did I attempt to intrude on them, but there is no doubt in my mind that many of our Light Sussex cockerels ended their days in that cave as sacrifices to the gods.

The subject of *curandeiros* interested me, especially when Benedito told me one day that they could be from any walk of life and that the genuine ones never charged for their services.

'There are several charlatans about', he said darkly, 'but the good ones can cure your cattle by blessing them and even bless your toothache better. They have real healing powers, which they place at the service of the community without charge.'

Once, when a *curandeiro* was visiting our farm, I told him about the trouble we were having with large numbers of rattlers, corals and other poisonous snakes, which were a constant danger to human and animal life.

'Let me know at once if anyone is bitten and I will soon fix it', he said.

I asked him what the treatment would be.

'Quite simple', he replied. 'The first thing is to call all the snakes in order to discover who the culprit is. I would summon them to your coffee-drying yard, get them lined up and ask which snake had bitten my friend. The guilty snake would then wriggle forward from the line. I should then tell him to go up to you or to whoever had been bitten and he would sink his fangs into the wound and suck the poison out. There would be no trouble after that from the bite.'

I promised to keep his kind offer in mind but did not confess that I personally would never have the courage to go through such a performance, however convinced I might be that the process would be effective. There are so many amazing cures carried out by these *curandeiros* that it is difficult not to believe in them. An Irish friend of ours in Brazil was losing several horses every month on his farm through snakebite and finally in desperation called in the local *curandeiro*. This gentleman burned some feathers, intoned a few incantations and pronounced the case solved. Our friend declared it as a fact that he never saw a snake again on his farm. His neighbour complained bitterly, however, because they all migrated to his property.

A deep affection for Brazil, gained from spending my childhood years there, was confirmed and increased during those pleasant days at Atibaia, and I had no thought to the future other than to continue farming forever.

I got on well with the inhabitants of our secluded corner of the Brazilian countryside and was treated by them with unfailing courtesy and kindness. They called me merely 'The Englishman' and no doubt thought I was a trifle mad to live by choice far from the city fleshpots. We were all concerned with our local problems and paid little heed to happenings in the outside world. Not having watched the war-clouds gather, I was profoundly shocked when war broke out in September 1939. I happened to be at the Mickey Mouse restaurant in São Paulo during one of my infrequent visits to the big city when the news came through, and the announcement over the radio left me stunned. It seemed incredible that my country was now at war with another. One read about wars in books but did not expect to get personally involved in them. I rushed to the British Consulate as soon as it opened the next morning and found myself in a queue with many others who felt that England could not do without their services. The Consulate merely put a stamp in our passports saying, 'Registered for the year 1939' and told us to do nothing for the moment, an attitude which left us all with a feeling of terrific anti-climax. As the weeks dragged by, we became firmly convinced that the war would be over before we got home to join up; the thought struck us as most unfair.

It was not until the first half of 1940 that those of us who had volunteered our services at the Consulate were told to report for medical examinations. It was just my luck that the person conducting them should be our family doctor. Nicely but firmly, he turned me down flat, because he knew only too well that I had mastoid trouble and no eardrum on one side. Other British Latin American volunteers were sent home at government expense to fight for King and Country, while I fumed and fretted. It was impossible to settle down to farming while there was a war on, a war that was not going too well for us at that time. Eventually, my father came up trumps and paid the passage for me to travel home by ship as a private individual. Having served in the 1914–18 war, he clearly understood my anxiety to join up in this one. We said goodbye at the gangway of the Highland Princess in Santos, and he made me gulp a bit by telling me, 'I'm proud that you are going.'

Life on board was very different to leisurely peacetime voyages out to Brazil and back for the school holidays. Everything was blacked out, and we all had to do regular submarine watches by night and day on the boat deck. Lifebelts had to be carried at all times, together with a small emergency case containing the cherished possessions you would like to save in the event of being torpedoed and taking to the boats. I solemnly lugged my saxophone around with me day and night, until the weight began to tell and I replaced it with a packet of Players cigarettes. This decision was welcomed with obvious relief by those fellow passengers who had been unfortunate enough to hear me trying to play my only tune, which was 'Over the Rainbow'.

Nearly all the passengers were official volunteers, mainly male, and most of them came from the Argentine. The ones I remember best were Jimmy Traill, Bobby Kent and Jack Rumball. Jack, like myself, was a fare-paying passenger, since he had been declared medically unfit because of some heart condition. He was the life and soul of the party and kept us all amused throughout the voyage. His impersonation of Carmen Miranda, in particular, was an absolute riot. This was carried out in improvised costume on top of a smoke-room table, and at the critical moment a huge feather in his headdress invariably got caught up in the ceiling fan. This part of the act always brought the house down.

These demonstrations of youthful high spirits helped us to forget the immediate dangers and those that lay before us. We saw no U-boats and, suffering from nothing more serious than hangovers, we sailed one night in November 1940 into Avonmouth in the middle of a heavy air raid. I stood on the top deck watching the guns blazing and the bombs exploding and felt suddenly sobered by the reality of war. It also struck me as monstrous that the Germans should have attacked the city on the very night of our arrival. After all, to be killed before even joining up would have been too awful for words.

Chapter 2

Joining Up

It was a strange experience arriving in a blacked-out London for the first time, and it amazed me that my taxi driver was able to get from Paddington station to the Cumberland Hotel with practically no lights at all. I stayed at this hotel on many later occasions, not only because it was cheap in those days but also because its solid concrete construction made me feel that only a direct hit during an air raid would make any real impression on it. Londoners were now enduring their long ordeal by bombing; the Luftwaffe had switched to night raids about two months previously, when the Battle of Britain ended. Nobody in the hotel showed any of the nervousness I felt, however, and only the uniforms here and there showed that this was not peacetime.

While wandering round the streets the next day I heard the wail of an air raid siren for the first time, and its notes had barely died away before I was in the depths of a shelter, only to re-emerge somewhat sheepishly when no one else joined me there. I never went into a shelter again during the war.

Having been away from England for four years, there was plenty for an impressionable twenty-one-year-old like myself to see and do, and it was a matter of only five days before my slender means began to run out. The fun was over, and now it was time to join up. Pangs of hunger finally overcame my desire for musical expression, and I sold the saxophone to a shop in Shaftesbury Avenue. The wonderful breakfast I had immediately after the sale on some of the proceeds will live long in my memory.

My original intention on leaving Brazil had been to try for the Scots Greys on the strength of an introduction to their Colonel, but my inquiries revealed that the Regiment was away in Egypt and equipped with tanks, not horses. So it seemed to me that in spite of the Gatwick experience I was cut out for flying. I therefore presented myself at the Air Ministry as a candidate for the Royal Air Force Volunteer Reserve and was quickly put into the machinery of recruitment. All went well until I got to the medicos. Here you had to do what was called 'blowing up the mercury'. A clip was put on to your nose and you then puffed into a tube, which registered pressure in degrees. A certain minimum pressure had to be held for a period of fifty or sixty seconds. Fifteen seconds was my best effort, and things began to look desperate. The doctor then advised me to take several deep gulps of air before puffing, and the improvement in performance was miraculous. I huffed and puffed for seventy seconds without any difficulty before being told to stop. It was wonderful to have passed this test, but what it proves has never been clear to me.

My successful progress through the medical fields came to a halt in the ear sector. The hearing tests were quite easy to fiddle, since my right ear is exceptionally good. However, the harassed young doctor was not to be fooled when he inspected the inside of my defective lug.

The greatest gloom came over me when he said, 'You had better get treatment for it at an ear hospital for about ten days and then come back and see me.'

It looked very much as though I was going to be pipped at the post. Quite apart from anything else, my money could not possibly keep me for another ten days. After getting my ear filled with powder at a hospital, I presented myself two days later to the same Air Ministry doctor.

'This is all rather puzzling', he said after a long examination. 'With all this powder I can't see much but it appears to me that you either have a thickened eardrum or no eardrum at all. Since you've come all the way from Brazil, I'll pass you for flying, although probably I shouldn't.'

Bless him; no words could have made me happier. After being recommended for aircrew, I was told to report on 2 December 1940 to Number 1 Receiving Wing at Babbacombe in Devon, where the business was to start. Things were beginning to move in the right direction.

All of us raw recruits at Babbacombe were unused to a military way of life and we found everything very baffling at first. Orders to report immediately for a 'FFI' had us gaping like ignorant rustics, and it became no clearer when a belligerent Warrant Officer told us that this was a 'short arms inspection'. In the welter of uniform and kit issues we could not remember having been given any weapons, but the mystery was soon solved when we found ourselves lined up with our most vulnerable parts bared to the critical view of a medical officer to check that we were 'free from infection'. We were all now dressed in ill-fitting uniforms and uncomfortable new boots as AC2s, or Aircraftsmen Second Class, but there was nothing very martial about our bearing. I constantly forgot my service number, and it was a long time before 1382508 became as deeply engraved on my memory as it was on the fireproof identification disc worn round my neck. Most of us were reeling from repeated vaccinations and injections of every kind, the effects of which had us groaning on our straw-filled palliasses during the little off-time we were allowed. In spite of it all, we learned to queue up for our food with 'irons' (knife, fork and spoon) and to line up in alphabetical order to receive our AC2s' pay of half-a-crown a day. It always struck me as an injustice that the W's should be pretty well last to be paid, but my suggestion that the changes should occasionally be rung by starting with the Z's fell on unsympathetic ears.

The effect of the injections, together with the bromide allegedly put in our tea, kept most of us from cocking an eye at the girls in Devon. However, there were those hardier souls among us who were unaffected by even these stunning blows. Their exploits and those of their supermen predecessors at Number 1 Receiving Wing served as the inspiration for a bawdy and unprintable song which started off, 'As she walks along the Babbacombe Road' and ended up with 'The girl who dared to join the Royal Air Force'.

After an uncomfortable three weeks at Babbacombe we were posted to ITWs (Initial Training Wings). I went to Number 5 ITW in Torquay on 20 December 1940. This was installed in what had once been a comfortable hotel, but there was no similarity between our life there and that of the guests who had patronized it in peacetime days. We slept four or more to a room on narrow iron beds with palliasses beneath us and thin blankets above. Our miseries were added to by a misguided medical officer with strong views about health and fresh air who decreed that our doors and windows should be permanently nailed open to let in the winter breezes. His orders were rescinded only after someone developed pneumonia. We got up at an ungodly hour and, after a hasty breakfast, formed up as a squad and marched through the dark streets to lectures, with hurricane lamps at the head and tail of our grumbling procession. We attended lectures on mathematics and lectures on navigation, and it was like school all over again. Between lectures, we did squad drill and occasional ten-mile runs in bitterly cold weather. Weekly kit inspections were an ordeal, since everything had to be laid out on our beds in mint condition, the centrepiece of the arrangement being a pair of boots upside down with their soles nicely polished. The food, which was not bad, was never quite enough, but whenever we complained that we were as hungry as hunters, the reply came that we were eating balanced rations. The awful decision had to be taken whether to spend our pay of half-a-crown a day on beer and cigarettes or on egg and chips; more often than not, we went for the food. At the end of a hard day we often had to do guard duty all night, which entailed a duty period of standing with a rifle at the road entrance to our billet and challenging all comers. There was no question of any time off in lieu the next day.

Square drill was desperately hard work, and anyone making a mistake was severely punished. After doing something out of step one day, I had to do fifty press-ups in the snow while the rest of the squad went off to lunch. I got none. We marched at the fast RAF rate of one hundred and forty paces to the minute, and Flight Sergeants beside us carried measuring sticks to check periodically that our paces were the regulation length. Altogether it was utter hell, but we thrived on it nevertheless and began to look less like a rabble. Surprisingly, we put on weight, and this must have been solid muscle. The whole programme was designed to lick us into shape and, although we often complained bitterly that we had joined the RAF to fly and not to march one hundred and forty to the minute, it is clear in my mind that we were being taught the essential quality of discipline, without which no fighting service can operate successfully. We soon learned the ropes, and experience taught us that a request for volunteers interested in driving fast cars would result in the eager acceptors being detailed to move a heavy item of equipment from A to B in double quick time. A discreet silence now enveloped us when volunteers were called for, but our Flight Sergeant could always fall back on the old routine of 'I want three volunteers; you, you and you'. It was not policy to argue with Flight Sergeants.

One day we were told that a new Flight Sergeant by the name of Matthews was to take charge of us. This information was accompanied by so many guffaws and full-of-meaning asides that it was apparent to even the most backward, out-of-step, mentally deficient and awkward bunch of cretins who made up a squad in the RAF that something remarkable was about to happen to us. We had not long to wait, and our nervous fears were fully justified when Flight Sergeant Matthews descended on us like a wolf on the fold, or rather like a full-blown hurricane hitting a half-put-up-tent in Florida. We were sitting lethargically in our lecture room when Matthews walked in, a pouter pigeon of a man with a great air of authority about him. We were cowed into silence while he walked slowly round the room, viewing us interestedly from every angle. Finally, with a snort of the deepest contempt, he swept out, leaving us all looking at each other with a sense of dread. His performance would have put any actor from the days of silent films into the shade for sheer dramatic effect. We began to twitter nervously among ourselves about the future course of our lives at Number 5 Initial Training Wing.

We did not wait long to find out. Flight Sergeant Matthews really put us through the hoop. His stream of invective during ground drill was a thing of beauty and quite unequalled by anything we had heard before. It seemed hard that he should be saddled with such scum as ourselves on which to waste his valuable time. Sheer fright made us spring to with a will, but all our efforts to please him seemed unavailing. We apparently kept in step about as well as a centipede, and our outward appearance was simply frightful. Our legitimacy was also called into question many times.

One day, the squad was marched up as usual to the canteen where, on the final word of command, we fell out quickly with irons to get in the queue for food. On this particular day, some miscreant fell out at least two seconds before the word of command allowed him to do so, and Flight Sergeant Matthews was not prepared to let this crime go unpunished. We were immediately re-formed into a squad and told to report ten minutes later in full anti-gas clothing. This meant putting on a gas-mask and gas-cape, which were about the most uncomfortable things I have ever had to wear; the cape limited movement and the mask made breathing difficult. We then did forty-five minutes' drill at the double in full gas equipment, and by the end of it we were puffing like steeplechasers after a four-mile race. Our lunch was cancelled, of course. It really was the most killing exercise, and the fact that we did not slay Matthews on the spot, something dear to our thoughts, showed that we had begun to accept discipline and feel respect for authority.

On Saturday afternoons we paraded after lunch wearing the kit appropriate to the sport in which we intended to indulge during our afternoon off. The more athletic of us appeared in shirts, shorts and rugger boots. I used to turn up in tunic, breeches and riding boots, because there were some quite nice horses at a nearby riding school run by an attractive redhead. My sports dress never failed to excite the intense interest of Flight Sergeant Matthews. He would walk slowly round our squad several times and then stop in front of me, eyeing my outfit up and down with many an expletive harrumph. At last, when the nervous titters had begun to die away, he would draw himself up and order imperiously, 'Fall out, Lord Gort!' I then scampered away to the charming redhead, pursued by valedictory invective from the Flight Sergeant.

I managed to fox him on several occasions about ten-mile runs, however. We used to set off from our hotel billet dressed in the flimsiest of clothing during what was often a howling blizzard. A few scrimshankers and I would set a tremendous pace for the first mile, leaving all behind, including Flight Sergeant Matthews, and would then dart into a nice warm café, where we spent the next two hours playing snooker. The rest of the squad used to run past our café and complete the agonizing circuit while we lounged in warmth and comfort. When they reappeared, tired and frozen to the marrow, we would emerge from the café and take the vanguard, running strongly. We always arrived back first at our billet and thus got the hottest and cleanest baths before our exhausted and dejected companions stumbled in. It was not strictly cricket, but the competition of life was such that we experienced no qualms of conscience.

Our patience and physique finally began to break under the harsh tutelage of Flight Sergeant Matthews, and we even talked about shooting him. It would be easy, someone argued, for one of us on guard duty to bump him off. One night when Flight Sergeant Matthews returned at 23.59 hours, the sentry could merely say, 'Halt, who goes there?' and fire his rifle before the bane of our life had time to reply. At any subsequent inquiry, the assassin would state that the person challenged had acted suspiciously by not giving the countersign immediately. This was nothing but a dream and, needless to say, there was nobody prepared to carry out the foul deed.

We continued to be bullied unmercifully on the parade ground by Flight Sergeant Matthews until, lo and behold, we began to get in step and look less like a rabble. He eased up on us as soon as we marched and acted less like a shower of muck, and it was then that the revolutionary thought took hold of us that Flight Sergeant Matthews was perhaps rather a good fellow. We suddenly realized that he was in fact the salt of the earth, and by the end of the course we would all have willingly laid down our lives for him. He even complimented us one day on our drill, and this practically froze the squad in its tracks.

At the end of the course, our squad gave a party at the Drum Inn at Cockington near Torquay for Flight Sergeant Matthews and our Commanding Officer, a rather peppery Squadron Leader who had seen much service in India on the North-West Frontier. We were determined to get Flight Sergeant Matthews tight even if we died in the process. We must have been fairly successful, for I can at least recall a moment when he fell into the pub's large open fireplace, from which we at once extracted him with the greatest tenderness. We then moved on to the Spa Ballroom in Torquay, where our Commanding Officer finally passed out. We covered his snoring form with flowers from the table and the corpse to his home we hurried. When we arrived at his front door, his wife looked out of the window at the rather unsteady procession and said, 'Poor Percy, the malaria has got him again.' Agreeing quickly, we dumped the body and beat a hasty retreat. It was not a situation we wished to get involved in, but we hoped poor Percy would manage to carry it off.

With the course completed, the burning question was where we would be posted from here. A particular friend of mine left with a small group at short notice one morning and managed to discover before departure that their destination was Canada. I believe they actually went to the USA for training in Arizona under a scheme operated by the Americans for the RAF. Every morning, we hurried to the notice board to see whether there were any posting instructions for us. A small number of people from the squad, myself included, were never mentioned at all, and we became thoroughly alarmed at being left out of it when the rest of our companions went off to start the next stages of their training. At last the mystery was solved, when a notice was put up saying that we had failed our navigation and were condemned to do another ITW course. Our feeling of frustration was immense. On 6 March 1941 I moved to what had once been a lavish hotel in Paignton and started all over again with the same old drill and lectures, plus an extra one hundred hours of instruction in navigation. The only moment of real excitement we had at Paignton was one night when German bombers set fire to our billet with incendiaries. We were so browned off with training that we rather hoped the place would be burned to the ground, but in the event the fire services soon had things under control, and we went back to bed.

At the end of the course I passed the examinations by the skin of my teeth and was posted on 7 May 1941 to Number 8 EFTS (Elementary Flying Training School) at Woodley, near Reading. Finally the rigours of ITW square-bashing and bull were over and, God be praised, we were now actually going to learn how to fly. I packed my kitbag and set off with a light heart for Berkshire.

Chapter 3

Elementary Flying Training

Woodley was a very different kettle of fish to ITW as far as creature comforts were concerned; indeed, it almost seemed as if we had been projected into another world. We sprog pilots lived in the most acute comfort in a country house near the airfield with a Jeeves butler and a Mrs Beeton cook to look after us. The rooms were comfortable, and we sat down to meals at a polished table set with silver. It was as though we had moved from a condemned boarding-house to the Ritz.

On 8 May, the day after our arrival, I took to the air for ten minutes' flying experience in a single-engine two-seater low-wing training aircraft called the Milles Magister with Sergeant Moore, an ex-Battle of Britain pilot, who seemed an absolute hero to me. He was a gentle and sympathetic instructor, who gave me a great love for flying. Soon afterwards, I was taken over by another instructor called Pilot Officer Sproston, who trained me up to my first solo. His ability to preserve an absolute calm at all times gave his pupils great confidence, but I fear that my performance must have caused him some twitches of the stiff upper lip on many occasions. We ran through the whole gamut of climbing, gliding, stalling, medium turns, taking off into the wind, powered approach and landing, and spinning. I hated that long moment hanging on the prop at the top of a stall before going into a spin, and dreaded the next phase, when the earth started whirling round. At least the Maggie (as we called our aircraft) recovered very quickly when you kicked on opposite rudder and shoved the stick forward. It was all terribly difficult at first, and most of us despaired of ever going solo. One of my main faults was to over-correct any movement of the aircraft by excessively nervous movements of the stick and rudder. Pilot Officer Sproston soon cured me of this by pointing out that an aircraft should to a large extent be allowed to plough its way through the air just as a ship rolls and pitches through the sea.

'Ah', I said somewhat clottishly but with comprehension dawning, 'rather like riding a horse.'

'Yes', he replied understandingly. 'Ride it on a loose rein and don't keep jabbing at its mouth.'

This explanation helped me enormously, and after ten hours and forty-five minutes of dual instruction I was allowed to do my first solo flight.

Practically nothing one does in life for the first time can be so satisfying and exhilarating. One's first solo is unforgettable. You remembered to do the crosswind check properly; you turned into the wind after looking carefully all around, opened the throttles and suddenly found yourself airborne on your own without the comforting sight of the back of the instructor's head in the cockpit ahead of you. The loneliness is suddenly rather terrifying, and you begin to panic. But then a feeling of power comes over you as the aircraft responds to the controls just as it did when you were flying dual. By golly, I can cope, is the thought in your mind as you gingerly turn and bank over the airfield below. Now it is time to get back on to the ground in one piece, if only to stop your instructor pacing nervously up and down. The final approach is a bit unnerving as the ground gets closer and you try desperately to remember everything you were taught. Before, there was always that comforting and experienced hand to snatch you out of trouble when things were going wrong. Now you nervously wrench back the throttle and flatten off too high. The aircraft floats for an age, then there is a crunch and it is rolling safely on the ground. You made it. It may not have been a brilliant landing, but at least you have arrived. There was a saying that any landing you walked away from was a good one. The instructor looks relieved, and you cannot wait to tell your friends all about it.

Going solo was a flying training milestone in one's life, and there was a certain amount of niggling competition on the course about who went solo first. I am sure that laggards like myself were slightly jealous of our more expert companions who took to the air on their own in far less time than we did. A particular friend called Stanislaus simply could not make the grade, try as he would, and his face was a picture of sadness when he was finally taken off flying. Another pupil put up an astounding performance on his first solo. He had shown every aptitude for flying during his hours of dual, and the instructor soon sent him off on his own with every confidence. The pupil could not bring himself to close the throttle and land the aircraft. He came in perfectly to a few feet off the ground and then his courage failed him; open went the throttle, and round the airfield again he would go. This happened eighteen times, by which time he was in danger of running out of fuel. What his instructor was going through on the sidelines beggars description. Finally, the pupil made it in one piece, though somewhat shaken.

It was at Woodley that we first heard the nice if hoary old story about the flying instructor with something of a brutal approach to his pupils. When he thought a pupil was ready for solo he would suddenly remove the joystick from his cockpit, wave it ostentatiously and then throw it overboard. The pupil had no option but to land the aircraft. However, word got around. One day, when the instructor went through this routine, his pupil in the rear cockpit, giving every sign of wishing to follow his master's example, lost no time in removing the joystick from his cockpit and, with a carefree wave, throwing it overboard in the same way as the instructor had done. The panic-stricken instructor thereupon took to his parachute, while the pupil, who had taken a spare joystick on board for the show, proceeded to land at his leisure.

We were instructed in all aspects of the Miles Magister and got entries in our logbooks certifying that we understood the petrol, oil and ignition systems of the aircraft. Another rubber stamp certified that we had been instructed in airscrew swinging in accordance with the standard procedure as laid down in AP 129 (FTM Part I, Ch II, para 24) and AOC Reserve Command Instructions Number 9, Section 2. I cannot for the life of me remember what this meant, so it is probably just as well that I never had to swing a prop again.

Life in our country house billet was great fun, and we practically never went off on weekend passes to seek entertainment elsewhere. We had with us on the course two brothers called Smith from Trinidad who sang together in harmony with the true lilt of the West Indies. The rest of us could listen to them for hours. Their 'Ida, Ida, Sweet as Apple Cider' was the best version of this song I ever heard. The Smith brothers and I unintentionally committed a public nuisance once on a rare weekend outing to Marlow-on-Thames and were lucky not to be arrested. We thumbed a lift there and took a room for the three of us at a hotel in the town. Later that evening, we set off for a night on the Marlow tiles after locking the door of the room and absentmindedly pocketing the key. Unfortunately, we had left the lights on in the room and forgotten to draw the blackout curtains. Within a short time the police arrived at the hotel and had to batter down the door of our room in order to turn the lights off. Any infringement of the blackout regulations in those days was a serious matter, and the police announced they would return next morning to deal with the offenders. All this was told to us by the receptionist when we rolled back into the hotel later that night, and we accordingly departed very early next morning, which was perhaps not very public-spirited of us.

It was summer and the best time of the year to be flying from a weather point of view; I shudder to think what elementary flying training must have been like during the winter months. The best fun of all was low flying. It was only allowed in certain areas, but of course we went down to nought feet outside the permitted limits whenever there was a sporting chance of not being caught at this exciting game. However, penalties for breaking the rules were severe. There is the old story of the pupil who, accused of low flying in an area where it was not allowed, swore black and blue that he had never been below 3,000ft. A chicken taken from the air intake of his aircraft's engines was then placed as evidence before him, with the rather acid comment that it must have been some chicken to be flying at 3,000ft. There was no valid answer to such devastating logic.

One day I was taken up by another instructor called Pilot Officer Kelly, and he did some low flying that really had me hanging on to the cockpit. Two vehicles travelling in close formation on the ground below us drew him like a magnet. He shoved the nose down and we shot towards them at the rate of knots. Kelly obviously wanted to find out whether one wing of our aircraft would fit between the two. At the critical moment I became convinced that the space was too narrow but was proved wrong by an inch or two. The suddenly-caught reflection of myself in the aircraft wing mirror screaming my head off had a sobering effect, and thereafter I did my best to preserve a stoical calm throughout any Kelly performance. That man could really fly.

I thoroughly enjoyed elementary flying training but cannot claim to have been more than averagely good at it. Towards the end of the course, we had to undergo a flying test by Wing Commander Moir, the Commanding Officer, a rather dour and forbidding man in a black flying suit who had us all frightened to death on the ground in case we did anything wrong. The thirty-five minutes spent with him in the air during my test were petrifying, and he quickly lost patience with me because I simply could not hear his instructions through the speaking tubes.

'Line up on the blankety-blank.'

'Line up on the what, sir?' I replied ingratiatingly.

'On the sun, you idiot!' he roared.

I must have scraped through my test on a fraction, and I made a point of keeping out of Wing Commander Moir's way after that.

Having learned to get the aircraft off and on to the ground in more or less one piece, and to get around the countryside, we now embarked on aerobatics. After being given dual instruction on slow rolls, I immediately went up on my own and did eighteen of them off the reel. Alas, I never did one again in my life. Instrument-flying really appealed to me more than the uncomfortable attitudes of aerobatics, and instruction in the Link trainer, for instance, which most pupils loathed, simple fascinated me. The Link trainer consisted of a small fuselage mounted indoors; machinery activated it to simulate attitudes of real instrument-flying conditions. The pupil was totally enclosed in the cockpit, which was like that of a real aircraft, and had to work the stick and rudder pedals to fly the contraption on instruments as it ploughed its way through imaginary skies. The glamour of Spitfires and Hurricanes affected me strongly, but I was obviously not cut out to be a fighter pilot.

By the end of our course, I had completed twenty-five hours and forty minutes dual flying, thirty hours and fifty-five minutes solo and ten and a half hours Link trainer instruction. I was assessed as average. All of us pupils from the course were now fledgling airmen without wings. How we envied luckier mortals who wore that coveted emblem on the left breast of their tunics, and how difficult it seemed to be to qualify for that distinction. The only signs denoting that we were aircrew in the making were a white flash worn in our forage caps and all the assorted flying clothing with which we had been issued. I think it was at the end of the elementary flying training course that we were promoted to Leading Aircraftsmen and as such received a pay increase.

Woodley had been a very pleasant interlude, and the dangers of war had usually seemed far away. The creature comforts of our country billet, the good companionship, the airfield smelling as only English grass can in summer and the friendly pubs were all going to be hard to leave behind. It was with genuine regret that I left on 18 June 1941 to start the next course at 14 SFTS (Senior Flying Training School) at Cranfield in Bedfordshire.

Chapter 4

Senior Flying Training and First Operations

The discomforts of life at Cranfield came as a rude shock to us after the pampered existence at Woodley. There was no butler to minister to our needs; indeed, we had to queue up for food with knife, fork and spoon as in the old days at Babbacombe, Torquay and Paignton. The grub was often pretty nauseating, and 'lights' were a steady item on the menu. It was an awful comedown, and the only thing was to throw oneself into flying training without thought for the inner man. We trained on twin-engined Oxfords, which were not too easy to fly; any careless liberties taken with this type of aircraft could result in sudden death. However, we were encouraged to hear that one pilot had managed to belly-land an Oxford at full speed, even though the whole of one wing outboard from the engine had been sliced off when hitting a barrage balloon cable. A warning notice was stuck in our logbooks saying, 'An aircraft crashed through your carelessness or disobedience will divert workers from building fighters and bombers to repairing training aircraft.'

After going solo in daylight we did navigational and cross-country flights before getting on to the trickier business of night flying. This fascinated me and never failed to do so throughout my flying days. To roar off the runway between two lines of flares, to circle in darkness and then land the aircraft in one piece at dead of night was a most satisfying and exciting sensation. Flying by day seemed drab by comparison, except when it was low flying. There was a real danger from enemy night-fighters, called bandits, which circled training aerodromes in the hope, often realized, of catching sprog pilots doing shaky night circuits and bumps on first solo or training flights. The first indication we had that bandits were about was when the aerodrome lights were suddenly turned off. This never failed to send prickles down my spine. You felt like a lost soul with nowhere to go. If you circled the aerodrome or beacon there was a danger of getting shot down, and if you headed for the comfort of outer darkness you probably got lost. It was all very aggravating to have one's training interrupted in such rude fashion. I believe that one pupil pilot on his first night solo became so angry about being attacked at an awkward moment that he lost his temper and rammed the enemy fighter. They both crashed, and there were no survivors.

Our flying training continued with cross-country after cross-country, and these exercises undoubtedly stood us in good stead during later operational days. I well remember my first instrument-flying cross-country, which served to convince me of the merits of dead reckoning navigation. This consisted of drawing a straight line from A to B, called the track, and then laying off the course to steer, which compensated for the drift one expected to get from the estimated force of the wind. If the predictions of the weather prophets were wrong, you could get blown miles away from your destination. Bad flying could achieve the same result. Sergeant Cameron, my instructor, made me fly on a triangular route by dead reckoning and gave me no chance to look out of the cockpit. On the final leg, when we were just about due to be over the airfield, he asked me where I thought we were. Somewhat doubtfully, I replied that we should be arriving back at base. With his permission, I looked out and found that we were crossing the boundary fence of the aerodrome. This was sheer luck, but it convinced me that DR navigation had something. Thereafter I always believed in it and was never let down.

The course ended on 6 September 1941, and I was then commissioned as a Pilot Officer and, glory of glories, given my wings. A week's leave was thrown in to fill my cup of happiness. I rushed off to stay at the Overseas League in London and lost no time in ordering my uniform from a tailor. I wanted desperately to strut about in my wings. The delay was terrible, but eventually I was able to turn out in them. My chest swelled to such an extent with pride that the buttons of my tunic were in danger of flying off under the strain. I walked about on air, until brought down to earth with a bump by an official telegram informing me that at the end of my leave I was to be posted as a flying instructor to Flying Training Command. The thought of not becoming operational, especially after being given those lovely wings, was simply intolerable. Moreover, the business of instructing sprog pilots sounded far more dangerous than having a crack at Jerry. Better to be knocked down by enemy flak or fighters than be run into the ground by a pupil on his first circuit and bumps.

I reviewed my introductions to the higher echelons of the RAF and found only one. This was a card given me by an Irish friend in Brazil to an acquaintance of his called Dermot Boyle.

'He's something in the RAF', he had said. 'But I'm not quite sure what he does.'

It took quite a bit of research, but I finally ran Dermot Boyle to ground in the Air Ministry. He was a Wing Commander, nothing less than God to me as a very new Pilot Officer. He could not have been more charming when I found myself in his office. He sat in his chair with his feet relaxed on the desk and questioned me about my service in the RAF, swinging a key chain around one finger the while.

'Posted to Training Command?' he said. 'But that's all wrong. You've come all the way from Brazil and obviously want to go on operations. Now, what's it to be. Hurricanes, Spitfires or bombers?'

I could only make noises of subdued ecstasy in the face of such proffered delights.

'Bombers, I think', he said musingly, 'They are really worthwhile.'

I nodded mutely.

He picked up the telephone and got through to a very senior officer in the RAF. An exchange of crisp sentences followed, and then Dermot Boyle turned to me and said, 'Well. That's fixed. Stay on leave and disregard all postings until you get one to an Operational Training Unit.'

What a marvellous man. It was my supreme good fortune to meet him. When we met again nearly thirty years later, I was able to thank him once more for the great service he did me on that day in 1941.

I stayed on at the Overseas League and had enough confidence in Dermot Boyle to ignore a telegram which arrived one day posting me to Training Command. My conscience about staying on unauthorized leave became guiltier and guiltier as time went by, and I spent longer and longer settling my nerves at the bar in the company of newfound friends from the Norwegian Air Force. They seemed quite impervious to normal alcoholic drinks and were said to have a preference for a terrible concoction made up of half gin and half hundred-octane petrol. Those Norwegians seemed to have inherited iron constitutions from their Viking ancestors, and I found it difficult to keep going at their pace. During one evening session we were all dragged out from the bar of the Overseas League to take part, most reluctantly, in a radio quiz programme being recorded live in the building. The organizers clearly thought it would be nice to have some servicemen taking part but must have had regrets when they discovered what an unruly lot we were. There was a great deal of ribaldry and friendly badinage, which was suddenly cut short by the interviewer telling us that we were on the air. This silenced us effectively, and a desire for instant escape overtook us when we learned that the programme we were on was a spelling competition. I was the first victim.

'Spell rhododendron', said the interviewer.

I could not spell the word at the best of times, and this was not the best of times. My ineffectual beginnings of 'R-O-D-O' resulted in my immediate dismissal from the competition. My companions fared equally badly and had to retire ignominiously. Heaven knows what listeners must have thought of our performances. 'What a dissolute and illiterate lot these airmen must be', I could imagine them saying.

My nervous tension evaporated a couple of days later with the arrival of a telegram instructing me to report to 25 OTU (Operational Training Unit) at Finningley, near Doncaster. Calling down every kind of blessing on the head of Dermot Boyle, I set off happily for Yorkshire and the next stage of training for operations.

Finningley was a pre-war station, and its building provided us with a comfortable Mess and living quarters. Friendly WAAFs served good food to us and attentive stewards came to take our orders for drinks when we pressed bell pushes in the anteroom of the Mess. We lived well but had to work hard. After reporting for duty I was attached to No. 7 BATF (Blind Approach Training Flight) where I did about ten hours blind flying on Oxfords, a valuable experience. We pupils trundled Oxfords around Finningley aerodrome in broad daylight, but all sorts of devices, including special goggles, were used to simulate bad weather conditions. We flew on the Lorenz beam and listened to its messages in our earphones. Dots told us if we were to the left of the beam and 'dahs' indicated we were to the right of it. A peculiar 'boop-booping' noise meant that we were over the outer marker, where our height should be 700ft, and a 'beep-beep-beep', rather more urgent, said we were over the inner marker at the edge of the aerodrome, where we were supposed to be at 200ft and ready to make the final approach. The whole thing fascinated me. The system demanded human response and correct flying for results which could mean life or death in really bad flying conditions. My training stood me in good stead some time later, when I had to do a beam landing in thick fog after an operation. Many pilots hated BAT flying, but I loved it. One of our instructors had the system so well taped that he could feel his way down to the ground in an uncanny way and carry out a perfect landing.

After the blind flying training course was over, I flew Ansons for a few hours and quickly learned about the undercarriage procedure. To retract the gear involved 240 turns by hand on the appropriate control, a fatiguing business. One soon began to work out whether the total flight time justified the elbow grease necessary to get extra flying speed from having the undercarriage up. It was usually worth it if there was someone else to wind the handle, but usually not if you had to do this yourself.

Next came a few hours on Wellingtons, nice aircraft to fly, though earlier types were rather slow, and then back on to Ansons. The main progress we had made by this time was to get ourselves crewed-up. I am sure that the navigators, bomb-aimers, wireless-operators and air-gunners allocated to us sprog pilots looked at their designated crew captains with considerable nervousness. After all, we might be flapping our wings, but as regards operational flying, we were completely wet behind the ears. It says much for their keenness and morale that they endured some of those shaky training flights with us. Like us, they were still learning their trades, but the difference was that they had to place their lives in their pilot's hands. However ropy our flying may have been, I cannot recall one single crash occurring during training. The glazed look of fear began to disappear from the eyes of our crew members as we chalked up more and more flying hours together. Mutual confidence was established not only in the air but also on the ground, and the regular nights out we had at local pubs helped to weld us into a bunch of comrades-in-arms with a pride in being members of the same crew. Crew feelings were very strong in Bomber Command, and we liked to stick together. Whether crew members were commissioned or non-commissioned made no difference to our friendship for each other, and we were all on Christian name terms. Some outsiders criticized non-commissioned members of aircrew for an easy-going attitude towards authority on the ground, and it is perfectly true that many sergeant air-gunners failed to salute their officers with Guardsman-like precision when passing on a station or in town. However, as members of a crew in the air they were absolutely splendid, and where you wore your stripes had no bearing on the job in hand.

I was lucky to get crewed up with a thoroughly nice mob. My bomb-aimer/front gunner was Vin Harley, a commissioned Australian whom I liked enormously. We shared a room for a long time as well as the wonderful food parcels he received from home, which included tins of fruit salad laced with passion fruit pips. Like many Australians, Vin had a weakness for poker or any form of gambling. We stuck together right to the end of my operational flying career.

My navigator was Bim Bone, a bit older than the rest of us; he, also commissioned, had been working in the City of London before joining the Air Force. He was a nice, quiet person, and his navigation was most meticulous.

My wireless operator was Tich Webster and, as his nickname implies, he was rather small. He turned out to be an excellent artist, but more of this anon.

Nobby Naylor and Ned Needham, both North Country men, were my air-gunners, and these two sergeants seemed to be quite inseparable. Full of wit, they never failed to produce amusing commentaries, usually bawdy, to meet any situation.

We flew hard on our training and did air firing practice, high-level bombing, instrument flying and circuits and bumps. On evenings off we had satisfactory thrashes at pubs in and near Doncaster. We paid £3 for an old Morris, which became the crew car. Something was irrevocably wrong with its electrical system, and we pushed it much further than we ever managed to drive it. I think we eventually abandoned it in some remote place, where it had broken down for the umpteenth time.

In February 1942 we were moved to RAF Bircotes, a satellite airfield of Finningley, where we lived in secluded Nissen huts but had the satisfaction of being on Manchesters. These were beautiful aircraft to fly as long as their engines did not catch fire. We buoyed ourselves up with the thought that the famous Kipper Herring had managed to fly one back from Berlin on one engine, for which he received a well-deserved gong. The Manchester had two Vulture engines and in airframe design was the forerunner of the Lancaster. We did quite a lot of hours on this type and imagined that this was the aircraft in which we should finally carry out a tour of operations. These hopes seemed to be confirmed when we were posted at the end of the course to No. 50 (operational) Squadron at Scampton in Lincolnshire.

I read and re-read the notice, savouring every word of it. We were going to an operational squadron and would shortly be having a bash at the Third Reich. The nail-biting in Brazil, the first fears of flying, the ghastly food at Cranfield, these were all so much water under the bridge now that we were going to become operational. The very word 'operational' had exercised mystical influences on us throughout our training, and we were impatient to remove the stigma of being so far non-operational. Next day, the posting was cancelled.

The powers that be had decreed in their wisdom that we should go on Lancasters, because the Manchester was being withdrawn from service, and to prepare for this we were detailed to return to 25 OTU for a further 100 hours flying on Wellingtons. We failed to see the logic of all this and went back with an ill grace to Bircotes for more circuits and bumps, air-firing, instrument-flying, flare path approaches and practice bombing. Looking back, I can see that we were extremely lucky to get this extra crew training as a preparation for future operations, however annoyed we may have felt at the time about this apparently retrograde step in our programme.

It was winter and we were all cold and miserable. The comforts of the Mess did not match those of Finningley, but at least there were some convivial souls around to keep our spirits up. One of them was Babe Learoyd VC, and I made the mistake of keeping him company one evening in a serious beer-drinking session. His capacity seemed to be limitless, even when I weaved off unsteadily to my Nissen hut after consuming fourteen pints. I was subsequently told that Babe stayed on to drink twenty-eight pints without turning a hair.

In May 1942, the marvellous news came through that my crew and I were posted to 106 Squadron at Coningsby in Lincolnshire, which was then commanded by Guy Gibson. After reporting to the station we spent the first few days flying Manchesters, something we did not expect after being put back on Wellingtons in preparation for Lancasters. On 29 May, however, I finally flew in a Lancaster as a second pilot to a Rhodesian named Bill Picken, and the experience was memorable. The flight only lasted about one and a half hours but it was enough to convince me that the Lancaster was a magnificent aeroplane. Nothing afterwards ever changed my mind about this. You could throw it into the most unorthodox attitudes, often impelled by sheer fright, and it was always free of vice. The Lancaster did not swing on take-off like the Halifax, nor did it have the deadly stabilized yaw of a Hampden. It was a joy to fly under any conditions and never gave you any impression of heaviness, although it had four engines and weighed about thirty tons. It carried a crew of seven, consisting of bomb-aimer/front gunner, pilot, flight engineer, navigator, wireless operator, mid-upper gunner and rear gunner. Browning .303 machine guns were mounted in the front, mid-upper and rear turrets. These had only about half the range of cannon carried by enemy fighters and Flying Fortresses but were effective at night, when attacking aircraft had to come in really close for the kill. Altogether, the Lancaster looked and behaved like a tough and capable aircraft and it proved its worth again and again throughout the war when called upon to carry enormous bombs well in excess of the load for which it was originally designed. Although the Stirlings, Halifaxes and Wellingtons also did a great job as the 'heavies' of Bomber Command, the Lancaster was, in my view, the queen of them all.

It was only twenty-four hours after Bill Picken had given me those first dual circuits and bumps that I was detailed, on 30 May 1942, to fly on operations as second pilot to another Rhodesian pilot named Bill Whamond. Finally, this was it. My feelings were a mixture of fear and elation. The stigma of never having been on ops was now to be erased, but I must confess that the approach of zero hour gave me a nasty sinking feeling in the pit of my tummy. One had no idea of what it was like to fly over hostile territory through flak and fighters and, most worrying of all, of what one's reaction to the baptism of fire would be. It was not so much the thought of death that frightened me but fear of the unknown.

I sat with Bill Whamond and his crew during briefing and heard that the target was Cologne. A large map on the wall of the briefing room showed the route to the target, and red patches on it showed where we should find the flak defences. One after another, specialist officers told us about the bomb load, the operational plan and what to expect from the defences and from the weather. It all sounded terribly matter-of-fact, until a visiting senior officer, who I think was Sir Alec Coryton, then AOC (Air Officer Commanding) No. 5 Group Bomber Command, stood up to tell us that 1,000 aircraft would be taking part in the operation. For this was the first thousand-plane raid. Every available aircraft in Coastal Command, and even some from Training Command, had been pressed into service to make up a greater force than had ever been launched from the air against an enemy. The number of aircraft really symbolized the fact that the tide of bombing had turned and that we were now going to repay the Germans more than twofold in their own coin. Previously we had taken it, but now we were going to dish it out. Even seasoned operational crews at the briefing seemed to be impressed by the news that there was going to be such a large crowd on Germany that night, and I, as a sprog, felt glad that my first trip was to be on a big show.

We ate our operational bacon and egg supper in the Mess and were then driven to the Flight offices, where we collected parachutes, torches and other bits and pieces needed on the operation. Escape kit, which included money and maps, was already stuffed into our battledress pockets. Some crew members, notably gunners, carried pistols shoved into their flying boots. In their exposed gun turrets they had to wear electrically-heated flying suits, but the rest of us needed no more than battledress, flying boots and perhaps a thick sweater, since the heating system in the Lancaster was good. The only mark of identification we carried was a strip of leather with our name on it sewn over the left hand breast pocket of our battledress. Before flying over enemy territory we had to empty our pockets of letters, bits of paper or any single thing that might identify our unit to the enemy. We had been briefed that, in the event of capture after being shot down or crashing in enemy territory, we should in no circumstances give any interrogating officer more than our name, rank and service number. We also carried yellow inflatable life jackets called Mae Wests and yellow skullcaps for use if we crashed in the sea. Apparently, this colour could be more easily seen than any other by searching aircraft and ships.

Flight vans picked us up and then dropped crews off at the various dispersal points, where their ground crews waited for them beside the aircraft. Lancaster H for Harry, silhouetted against a lovely English summer's night, was waiting for us, and we climbed on board. After getting the thumbs-up signal from the ground crew, Bill Whamond started the Merlin engines, which burst into life with their typical dry, snarling, popping crackle. After testing the intercom system between all members of the crew and carrying out the other lengthy checks necessary before take-off, Bill gave the thumbs up signal to the waiting ground crew, who darted under the wings to pull away the wheel chocks. We started rumbling down the perimeter track towards the end of the runway in use, where other Lancasters were already getting in the queue for take-off. Within a few moments we were roaring down the flare path and then lurching off into the darkness. We had just one 4,000lb blockbuster bomb on board for delivery to Cologne. I sat in the right hand seat of the cockpit and kept quiet.

We soon left the coast of England, and not long afterwards I heard for the first time that phrase used by the bomb-aimer which was to become so familiar: 'Enemy coast ahead'. Searchlights were weaving about there, looking rather pretty in the darkness. We got across the coast without difficulty and continued on our way with no opposition from flak or fighters. It seemed to be a piece of cake. There was no question of searching for the target: Cologne was already a blaze of light. Many aircraft had bombed before us and had left a sea of fire as a beacon for later arrivals. Visibility was good, and we could see the city burning long before we got there. We approached the target area, and I found it a bit shattering to look down and see how much destruction was being caused. In RAF parlance, this was a wizard prang. I felt strangely impersonal about the fact that people down below were being mutilated and blown to bits. We were a bomber crew doing the job we had been briefed to do and were giving the enemy back some of his own medicine. I think most crews had a detached attitude to the results of their bombing, so far as the loss of human life was concerned, but the matter became much more personal when we had to fight it out with a Jerry Me 109 or Junkers 88 in some lonely corner of the sky. Bombing was a cold-blooded business compared with aerial combat in Hurricanes and Spitfires. Bomber crews usually knew they would be on operations about twelve hours before going into action, whereas the fighter boys generally found themselves in the heat of battle within minutes of being scrambled off the ground to meet the enemy. At this stage of the war, bombing was England's means of hitting back at Germany, and I do not believe that any of us who delivered the bombs felt compunction or remorse about the destruction we caused. What the Germans had done to Rotterdam and Coventry and to people in concentration camps was too fresh in our minds for us to feel any sense of pity. In any case, it is difficult to feel pity for an enemy when he is doing his best to shoot you down with fighters and anti-aircraft guns. However, these feelings grew with time and experience, and at the moment I was a sprog second pilot in a Lancaster over Cologne on my first trip.

'I'm starting the run-in now', said Bill Whamond over the intercom.

'OK', replied the bomb-aimer. 'There's no problem about finding the target tonight. Everything is as clear as a bell.'

We made our run-in to the aiming point and dropped our load without difficulty. Anti-aircraft fire was desultory by now, and we saw no fighters. We turned out of the target area and left the sea of flames behind us. Even from 100 miles away, we could still see the glow from burning Cologne.

After landing back at base we were collected by a Flight van, which drove us off to the Flight offices, where we left our parachutes and other flying equipment, and then to interrogation. Here crews were required to report on the operation and, judging by jubilant remarks like 'wizard show', 'tremendous prang', and 'absolutely bang on', it was clear that the raid had been a great success. After being debriefed, we returned to the Mess and sat down to a second operational supper. I felt a great sense of elation to have done my first operational trip and only regretted that my crew had not been with me to share the adventure. They had to wait until I was considered experienced enough to go as Captain.

The trip to Cologne had come at the end of the month, and I was therefore able to enter it up immediately in my logbook in the red ink denoting night-time operational flying. Logbooks were made up at the end of each month and signed by both Flight and Squadron Commander. The trip had lasted only four hours and twenty minutes, but that entry in red was, for me, the most important thing in my logbook. The first thousand-plane raid on Cologne was also about the most important event that had taken place in the history of bombing. Up till then, Bomber Command had carried out attacks on German targets with a hundred aircraft or so at a time, but the weight of such attacks, coupled with inaccuracy of bombing often caused by bad weather conditions in the target area, had failed to inflict really serious damage. Just over three months previously, on 12 February 1942, we had been completely humiliated when the German warships *Scharnhorst*, *Gneisenau* and *Prinz Eugen* sailed through the Channel and got away without any of our aircraft being able to hit them with a single bomb. Doubts were expressed about the desirability of building up a bomber force, and the wisdom of pursuing a policy of bombing was seriously questioned. Air Marshal A. T. Harris, who had become Commander-in-Chief of Bomber Command in February 1942, believed that a properly conducted bomber offensive could do a very great deal to win the war and he set about organizing this offensive with a strength of purpose and understanding of the problems which soon had a profound effect on the efficiency and morale of those serving in his command. He had the courage to commit his entire bomber force to the thousand-plane raid on Cologne in a bold move to show that a heavy and concentrated attack by bombers could cause serious destruction. Many would have felt beforehand that such a move was too risky, but in the event, Harris was proved right. The future of our bombing policy and of Bomber Command itself probably depended upon the success or failure of that raid on Cologne, and this is what made the operation such a momentous happening. Apart from its impact on Cologne and the Germans as a whole, the raid acted as a great morale-booster for British servicemen and civilians. We had never had anything like 1,000 enemy bombers attacking our cities, and the mere thought of what destruction the weight of such an attack could cause was stimulating, because it meant that, at this stage of the war, which had not gone well for us so far, we were in a position to hit the enemy hard, and clearly this was only the beginning. It was a welcome shot in the arm.

Two nights later, we set off to attack Essen on the second thousand-bomber raid. I was again flying with Bill Whamond in Lancaster H for Harry, and we were carrying another 4,000lb bomb. We had no problems except that the weather was cloudy and we could not see the target very well. Essen was always one of the most important targets because of the Krupps factory there, but it was a difficult place to find on dead reckoning navigation and visual identification. It was often obscured by cloud, and there were no handy landmarks like wide rivers to help pinpoint one's position for the run-in to the target. Many attacks were carried out on Essen in the early days of the war, and many lives were lost in the process, but the place did not get hit properly until later, when new navigational aids enabled crews to establish their position. It was always heavily defended, and one had to fly through about forty miles of very nasty and efficient flak defences to get at the city from any angle. One story told among bomber crews was that the large number of shot-down RAF bombers there were put into the Krupps factory at one end and came out as anti-aircraft guns at the other. We never went to Essen without believing that the trip was going to be hell, and it nearly always was. Essen was the strongpoint of the Ruhr, or 'Happy Valley' as it was called sardonically by bomber crews.

We had a fairly trouble-free trip this time and bombed from 15,000ft. It was always a great relief to get your bombs off, as the possibility of getting hit with a full load on board fully occupied our thoughts on every run-in to a target. There were constant reminders of this danger when less fortunate aircraft got hit and went up in a blaze of light. The burning bits drifted down, and one wondered whether any of the crew had got out in time. After flying through the defensive web and dropping the bombs, one's desperate preoccupation was to weave out again through the curtain of flak to the protection of darkness beyond the ring of defences. After that came the long haul to the French or Dutch coast, with night-fighters looking for us. The best moments of an operation were the re-crossing of the English coast, the landing back at base and the operational supper afterwards.

Having now done two operational trips as second pilot, I was considered experienced enough to fly over enemy territory as Captain of my own aircraft and crew. Before doing so, however, it was necessary for my crew and I to complete a conversion course on to Lancasters at Coningsby. Once again, we went through the routine of local circuits and landings, overshoot procedure, beam flying, air-firing practice, cross-country flying and night bombing practice. We completed all these exercises satisfactorily and were then allocated to A Flight, 106 Squadron, as an operational crew. Our Flight Commander, Squadron Leader Robertson, made us do more training; on 11 June 1942, for example, we were called upon to carry out a night cross-country flight round the British Isles carrying a 4,000lb bomb, which we had to bring back to base. The flight, which lasted eight hours and five minutes, took us to Southwold, Oxford, Frome, Okehampton, the Smalls Lighthouse, Chicken Rock, Stornoway, Ru Stoer, Stirling, Dumfries, Hexham, Lincoln and back to base. It was rather a boring exercise, but good for our navigation and crew training.

Finally, on the morning of 25 June 1942, our Flight Commander informed me that my crew and I were 'on' that night. The burning question every morning on an operational bomber squadron was whether ops were on or not that night. After breakfast, the crew captains gathered in their Flight offices with the Flight Commander and waited for the news to come through from Group to say whether the squadron was on or not. If on, then the squadron would be told how many aircraft they were to put on the operation. The next thing was to decide how many aircraft from A and how many from B Flight would be flying, and which crews would be required to fly. Captains detailed for flying operations that night carried out a NFT or Night Flying Test in the morning. You flew around with your crew for anything up to half an hour and tested everything in the aircraft. This was important, because your lives would depend on the engines being serviceable, the radio in order and the Browning machine guns in good firing condition. The senior member of the ground crew always presented the Form 700 to the Captain of aircraft for his signature before taking the plane; this showed what checks and work had been carried out on the aircraft. We had the greatest confidence in our ground crews and always knew that they had worked their guts out to get the aircraft up to scratch. There was a bond between us, we were usually on Christian name terms and we drowned our sorrows together at the local. They took a pride in the aircraft they serviced and worked unstintingly under often difficult conditions. It was always sad to see the faces of a ground crew when their aircraft and flying crew failed to return after an operation.

After the NFT came the long wait until take-off at night. Wondering what the target would be was the main subject of our thoughts, and various indications gave room for speculation. For instance, if each aircraft was to carry a heavy load of bombs and a small amount of fuel, then the target could easily be somewhere in Happy Valley. If orders had come through for a maximum fuel load of 2,154 gallons and a smaller amount of bombs, then obviously it was going to be a long trip, possibly to Italy. Orders to load APor armour-piercing bombs gave us the willies, because this almost certainly meant that we should be called upon to attack warships, which could be very nasty targets indeed. During the waiting period we always felt frightened and had butterflies in our tummies. Few pilots drank more than half a can of beer at lunchtime, because flying was quite an intricate business and we had to have our wits about us. We were usually too keyed-up to sleep, but it was helpful to rest on your bed until briefing time.

Operational supper, generally taken in rather a pensive silence, consisted of a fried egg, that richest of prizes in wartime days, and the corny joke was to ask your next-door neighbour at the table whether you could have his post-operational egg if he did not return from the mission. Soon afterwards, the Flight vans appeared to carry us off to the Flight offices, where we collected our parachutes, Mae Wests and other gear. Our ground crew awaited us at the dispersal point, using only blue torches for lighting, and it was all rather eerie as we climbed on board and took up our allotted positions in the aircraft.

Earlier, we had been briefed that the target was Bremen and that this was yet another thousand-bomber raid. We would be flying in Lancaster B for Beer, and our load was a 4,000lb bomb. I was in the enviable position of having two operations under my belt but could sense that my crew was slightly nervous, since this was their first raid. We checked all the systems and then taxied to the end of the runway, where we joined the queue of Lancasters waiting for instructions from RT control. After getting clearance, we trundled down the runway, took off and set course for the coast. We were soon over the North Sea and not long afterwards saw the enemy coast lit up by flak and searchlights. We weaved through the defences and got on our new course for the target. Soon we were flying through filthy weather, thick grey cloud which enveloped us and gave me the impression of being suspended in some unearthly vacuum; the comforting sound of our engines was the only contact with reality and the job in hand. Visibility was nil, and I had to fly on instruments, essential aids that seemed to negate what my senses told me about our altitude and forward speed. However, when you flew blind on instruments, you had to believe in them and not in your senses, otherwise you could stall or end up in a headlong dive. The thought of collision with another aircraft was constant, but there would be no time to avoid it in this seemingly impenetrable mass of grey murk if the fates were against us.

The weather got a little better in the target area, and Vin Harley, my Australian bomb-aimer, guided us in and dropped the bombs from 12,000ft. There was still a lot of cloud, but from our calculations we reckoned we must be over Bremen. My crew had behaved splendidly in difficult conditions on their first trip. Weather conditions at base were lousy when we got back, and Control therefore diverted us to a satellite airfield called Woodhall Spa. It was good to be back in one piece after our first operation together as a crew. Vin Harley, our navigator Bim Bone and I celebrated in the officers' Mess, and I feel sure that the other four members of the crew got down quite a quantity of beer in the sergeants' Mess. We spent the night at RAF Woodhall Spa and flew back to base next day.

What worried me during my first operations was that I simply could not sleep after them, no doubt owing to nervous tension. I believe that other aircrew suffered from the same problem. After landing back from an op we were taken off to interrogation, where mugs of steaming tea laced with rum were put into our willing hands. After de-briefing we had our post-operational breakfast, sometimes washed down with a pint of bitter, in the Mess. It was often four or five o'clock in the morning by the time we got to bed, and one felt exhausted enough to sleep for twelve hours. However, sleep would not come, and I used to toss and turn, thinking about the operation we had just completed. It was only after doing about ten trips that I reached the stage where I could get into bed and go out like a light until lunchtime.

The general rule was that aircrew could be required to fly on operations two nights running and then have the next night off. However, in practice we rarely flew as much as this, because either your crew was not put on to fly or else bad weather prevented operations. Equally, your aircraft might be unserviceable. Leave was lavish, and we got a week every six weeks.

Coningsby was a happy and comfortable station, and I have the pleasantest memories of it. The Mess and other buildings had been constructed in peacetime and provided all comfort. The food was good, and there were charming WAAF waitresses to serve it, as well as efficient batmen and Mess stewards to minister to our needs. We made the most of this pampered existence, especially as none of us knew how long we should live to enjoy it.

The station was then a grass airfield with no concrete runways, located in the Lincolnshire countryside about 14 miles from the town of Boston, famous for its stump and large number of pubs. Was it a hundred and thirty-seven? I cannot remember the exact number, but there were few we did not visit during our nights off. The important thing was not to miss the last bus back, which left Boston at 11.00 pm and got us to the gates of the station in time to check in at the guardroom before the permitted deadline of 2359 hours. Arriving later than this meant that you were put on a charge and hauled up before the Squadron Commander. There was an amusing incident when one aircrew sergeant had several beers too many in Boston one night and missed the last bus home as a result. Wondering what on earth to do, he walked round the main square, which was in utter darkness. This was of course the time of the blackout and the period when there were scares about the possible invasion of England. Any vehicle left unattended had to be immobilized, usually by removing the distributor arm, in order that its use should be denied to an invading enemy.

During his unsteady perambulations round the main square of Boston, our Sergeant's eye suddenly lit on a Green Line bus standing lonely and unattended. Showing considerable initiative, he climbed into the driver's seat and pressed the starter button. The motor roared into life. It will always be a mystery how he managed it in his condition, but the Sergeant drove that bus to Coningsby and left it outside the guardroom. He checked in before 2359 hours by the skin of his teeth and retired to bed. Next day, of course, there was all hell to pay when the Green Line Company finally tracked down their bus to RAF Coningsby. They obviously wanted not only their bus back but also the blood of the person who had pinched it.

Things might have been serious for the Sergeant had it not been for our adjutant, Squadron Leader Martin, a downy bird with a Military Medal from the First World War and many years' service in the Forces. Clearly believing attack the best form of defence, he adopted a splendid line, which went more or less as follows: there was our Sergeant having a quiet beer or two in Boston on his night off. All very right and understandable, because aircrew undergo considerable strain and need a bit of relaxation once in a while. He was fully aware of the importance of catching the last bus back in order to check in at the guardroom at the appropriate time. However, on his way to the bus stop, our Sergeant suddenly saw an unattended Green Line bus in the main square. Being a responsible non-commissioned officer, his first thought was naturally to investigate whether the vehicle had been immobilized in accordance with standing regulations. His only way of checking this was by getting into the driver's seat and trying the starter. When the engine fired, it was clear that the owners of the bus had disobeyed regulations, thereby endangering the safety of the realm. The Sergeant's immediate thought was that the bus should be taken to a safe place, and the safest place he could think of was, understandably, the guardroom at his RAF station. He therefore drove it in the national interest to Coningsby and left it outside the guardroom. The Green Line Company found this argument quite unanswerable and were content to take their bus away without further complaint. Having saved the day for the Sergeant, the adjutant gave him a tremendous rocket and left it at that.

During that glorious English summer we received many kind invitations to visit people living in the neighbourhood of Coningsby, to play tennis or just to spend a quiet evening with them. During our off-time there was never a dull moment, since we often had parties in the Mess at which we were able to repay some of the local hospitality we had received. These parties were pretty gay affairs and usually ended up with the officers playing such athletic games as high cockalorum or indoor rugger. Another favourite was trying to jump over easy chairs from a standing start. The more expert drinkers qualified as members of the so-called Hangar Club by drinking a pint of beer while hanging upside down by their feet from a beam. It was all high spirits, but the Mess stewards must often have cursed us for the scene of devastation we left them to clear up next morning. It was an attitude of eat, drink, and be merry for tomorrow we die, although strangely enough, I think that most of us felt, 'It can't happen to me.'

We had some thoroughly good types on 106 Squadron. It happened that eleven new crews, mine included, were all posted there at the same time from the OTU where we had trained together, so there were lots of familiar faces around. Alas, after three months my crew of seven were the only survivors from those seventy-seven bodies. The chop rate was heavy in Bomber Command, but on a squadron you did not and could not afford to think about it. You felt a tremendous sense of regret when friends did not appear at the post-operational breakfast because they had gone missing on the operation, but there was nothing you could do about it. During de-briefing it had been easy to see the gaps on the blackboard. Against M for Mother, for instance, there was the crew list and take-off time, but a horrible blank space for the time of landing. When sufficient time had elapsed, it was clear that they were not coming back. They could have been killed or taken prisoner, or might have ditched in the sea. Sometimes, but not very often, we got news that an overdue crew had landed elsewhere because of mechanical trouble or as a result of being shot up. We rejoiced in such cases to know that they were safely back in England.

The Captains of my vintage whom I remember best were Taffy Evans, Bunny Grein (lost on 11/12 August 1942) and Rex Butterworth (killed on 2/3 October 1943). Rex and I shared a room, and he was really a disturbing person to live with because of his passion for Russian roulette. Most evenings, he would put one bullet in his revolver, spin the chamber and then pull the trigger with the muzzle against his head. This performance always worried me to death, but Rex maintained that the weight of the shell caused it to fall to the bottom of the chamber out of harm's way. While lying on my bed one evening I remonstrated with Rex, but he replied that there was no danger. To prove his point, he aimed the gun at the wall and pulled the trigger. It went off with a tremendous bang, and the bullet bounced round the walls and hit me on the knee. No serious damage was done, but I had a bruise from the spent round. Rex was sufficiently shaken by the incident not to play this dangerous game again.

Music was a great relaxation for us, and we wore out records of the peerless Glen Miller and his band. His style may perhaps be considered corny nowadays, but in those times his music contained, for us, just the right mixture of tunefulness and sentimentality. The Warsaw Concerto also holds very nostalgic memories for me. In particular, I remember one evening when Guy Gibson and a group of us were invited to dine in the WAAF officers' Mess. Afterwards we all sat on the floor with the lights turned out and listened again and again to the Warsaw Concerto. The music seemed to express all the poignancy of war, the comradeship, the times of happiness and the moments of fear and sadness. I can never hear the Warsaw Concerto without immediately thinking of life on an operational squadron.

Chapter 5

Hamburg

It was 26 July 1942 and the squadron was put on operations that night. My crew was detailed to fly and so we did the usual thirty-minute NFT in Lancaster J for Johnnie during the morning and tried to get some sleep in the afternoon. I had been very pleased when the Flight Commander gave me J for Johnnie, serial number R5749, which was a brand new aircraft just delivered to the squadron. I felt unhappy about this forthcoming trip, however, and had a nasty feeling that we might be 'going for a Burton' tonight. In RAF Bomber Command language this meant going missing on operations; the less euphemistic expression often used was 'getting the chop'.

My crew for the night's operation consisted of Bim Bone, my regular navigator, Tash Goodwin, the flight engineer, Tich Webster, the wireless operator, Johnny Cunningham, a sergeant bomb-aimer/front gunner standing in for Vin Harley, who was sick, and the rear and mid-upper gunners, Ned Needham and Nobby Naylor. All good men and true.

My batman woke me at 1745 hours and, after pulling on my battledress, I went off to briefing at 1830 hours with a sinking heart. On entering the Nissen hut where the briefing took place, my eyes turned automatically to the operational map on the board, where a line showed the route from base to target and back again. Hamburg was the target. My heart twitched; this was a very nasty target, and the flak there had a high reputation for its accuracy and strength. I sat down with my crew, and Tash expressed all our feelings quite unprintably. We listened with other crews to details of the bomb load, weather forecast, enemy defences and so on.

'J for Johnnie will bomb at zero plus two.'

Lost in my thoughts, I heard the words dimly, but suddenly the implication hit me like a cold shower. God Almighty, four aircraft from the squadron were starting the attack at one-minute intervals from zero hour! That meant that each of the four would be over the target completely alone for one minute before the weight of the attack was started by the main force of bombers. This sounded like murder. Hamburg was a hotly defended target, and just the thought of being over it alone for one whole minute made my blood run cold. We usually tried to saturate the defences by concentrating a large number of bombers on to the target in the shortest possible time. The German flak defences were said to be able to deal with six attacking bombers at a time and to have a good chance of shooting those six down. The simultaneous arrival of a large number of aircraft made it possible for many of them to get through, while the unfortunate six engaged the full attention of the enemy guns. A single bomber flying alone over Hamburg for a whole minute would be the target of every flak gun available. I felt an irresistible desire to go to the bathroom.

Back in the Mess, I went through the drill of preparation for flying. After putting on battledress, a sweater and flying boots, I placed a lucky bit of flak in my inside pocket, stuffed a torch into my right boot and removed all marks of identification other than my name over my left breast pocket. What had I forgotten? My mascot, the toy Koala bear given me by my Australian bomb-aimer Vin which went with us on every trip. All too soon, it was time for our operational bacon and egg supper, and shortly afterwards the transport arrived to take us to the Flight offices.

It was already dark, and activity in preparation for the night's operation was intense. We collected our parachutes and other gear while smoking one last cigarette after another. Our Padre, a nice man, was there to give us encouragement through his presence rather than by the use of unnecessary words about being ready to meet our Maker. As crews went to their aircraft, we exchanged the customary Bomber Command words of farewell: 'Have a good trip and see you at interrogation.'

'Enemy coast ahead', said Johnny calmly over the intercom.

Our take-off had been all right, and everything seemed to be working properly. A cone of searchlights suddenly pinpricked the darkness ahead, and heavy flak started firing at the intersection of lights. That was probably Taffy having a bit of trouble ahead of us, since he had been briefed to bomb at zero plus one. The aircraft coned in the searchlights weaved desperately from side to side like a moth caught in a lampshade. Now the light flak came up at us in coloured curves as though squirted from a hosepipe. It curved up lazily and then whipped past us at incredible speed like hail past a car windscreen. It was pretty stuff, but lethal. We got through unscathed and pressed on to the target. I kept weaving, because alterations in height and course made it more difficult for the ground flak to hit us. With their radar aids, the enemy worked out our height, course and speed and fired their anti-aircraft guns at our predicted position in so many seconds, allowing for our forward speed on a particular heading and the time it took for the shells to come up and burst. You saw the flash of the gun on the ground and quickly weaved in order not to be in the predicted position at which it had been fired. Weaving also helped us to keep a good lookout for enemy fighters coming up under the belly of the aircraft. The German night-fighters often worked in pairs. One stood off out of range to hold the attention of our air-gunners, while his partner crept up underneath and raked the bomber from stem to stern. Many unsuspecting crews must have got the chop in this way.

It was a clear night and we could see the target ahead of us, as well as the reception awaiting us there. Taffy must be getting it in the neck. The Germans had made tremendous efforts to camouflage Hamburg, even to the extent of building an artificial lake to mislead our bombers, and in view of this, we had been briefed to make absolutely sure of our aiming point before releasing the bombs, especially as the main force was to follow us. We started our run-in at 15,000ft and quickly began to get the full benefit of Hamburg's defences. Every gun on the ground seemed to be firing at us, and puffs of black smoke from heavy flak started to appear close to our Lancaster. They were too close for comfort, but there was no way round this heavy barrage.

'Over to you now, Johnny', I said to the bomb-aimer. 'We don't want to hang around the target area. Make sure you get your pinpoint at the beginning of the run-in.'

'Bombs fused' replied Johnny. 'Steady now, we're just about right. Left, left, steady. Hold her there.'

The sinister black puffs were all around us, and I began to sweat. Christ, there was no way of getting away from this stuff! It was all around and in front of us.

'No mistakes, Johnny. You damned well get those bombs off on the aiming point at the first time of asking or I'll never buy you a pint again.'

'Left, left, skipper, that's perfect', replied Johnny as he crouched over the bombsight.

My stomach muscles contracted as the flak burst close to us. Suddenly there was a tremendous crash and a blue flash followed by a sound like the tinkling of breaking glass. Out of the corner of my eye I saw Tash lurch backwards into the navigator's compartment. At the same time, the aircraft went into a dive and I struggled to regain control by winding back on the trimmer and jiggling with the revs and boost levers. We flattened out after losing a lot of height, but the aircraft seemed to be a bit sluggish on the controls. However, we were still flying. I called up the crew.

'Johnny, are you OK?'

'I've been hit, skipper, I can feel the blood running down my leg.'

'Have you got the bombs off?'

'I've tried, skipper, but they won't bloody well go. Something in the system must have gone for a Burton. I've tried jettisoning but they still won't go. I'm coming up to give you a hand.'

Johnny appeared out of the bomb-aimer's compartment in the nose and dragged himself on to the flight engineer's seat next to me. Raising a thumb he said, 'Don't worry, skip, I can cope.'

'OK, Bim?'

'I'm OK, skipper, but Tash has copped one in the neck. I've put on a bandage, am giving him a shot of morphine, and he's now on the rest bed.'

'Well done. What about you, Tich?'

'I'm all right, skipper', came the cheerful reply.

'Ned and Nobby?'

'Yes, OK, skipper'.

We were still over the target and being shot at right, left and centre. Things were not too happy, as the starboard outer engine appeared to have something wrong with it and was not producing full power. We managed to weave into comforting darkness outside the target area and away from that terrible flak. I was beginning to feel better, when suddenly Nobby called me up on the intercom.

'Skip, skip! We've flipping well had it! The starboard wing petrol tanks are on fire.'

My heart missed a beat as I looked out and saw tongues of flame licking out of the starboard wing. The whole lot could explode at any moment. My first reaction was to tell everyone to bail out, but all of a sudden I felt a reluctance to abandon the aircraft while it was still flying. And, incongruously enough, I thought how cold it would be to float down on a parachute. We might get lynched on landing or spend the rest of the war in the bag as prisoners of war. I decided not to bail out just yet.

There was nothing heroic about this decision. I just did not want to abandon the aircraft, which was our only means of getting back to England. Flying with the fire in the wing and the expectation of blowing up at any moment was nerve-wracking, but somehow I felt that the worst was not going to happen. The fire seemed to be getting worse, and we must have been clearly visible to the defences. I felt a sense of hopelessness when Johnny called up to say that the oil pressure on the starboard outer engine had dropped to nothing. I feathered it and flew on three at about 7,000ft. Our full bomb load was a nuisance, and I longed to get rid of it in order to improve the Lancaster's performance. However, some defect in the system meant that we were stuck with the lot.

We were like a sitting duck with the fire in the wing to give our position away. The danger now was from fighters, which usually liked to hang around on the edge of the target area and attack bombers as they came out of the flak barrage. There was no need to tell my crew to keep a sharp lookout for enemy fighters; we all knew the danger and felt a keen desire for survival. There was dead silence for five minutes.

'Look out, skipper!' cried Ned suddenly from the rear turret. 'Enemy fighter dead astern, about 600 yards.'

A feeling of desperation came over me as I waited tensely for further news from Ned. We were really getting the lot tonight. At such moments pilots relied implicitly on their gunners, and the survival of the whole crew depended on correct instructions being given by the gunner to the pilot at exactly the right second. Crew drill, boring when practised under simulated conditions, could now pay dividends.

'He's coming in. Prepare to turn to port.'

My hands were clammy as I gripped the stick and waited for cannon shells to come ripping into the Lancaster. Time seemed to stop.

'Prepare to turn to port. Go!'

I immediately threw the aircraft to port in the tightest turn possible, thereby making a deflection shot difficult for the fighter. My rear guns rattled and the acrid smell of empty .303 casing floated up the fuselage.

'I've got him, I've got him!' cried Ned excitedly over the intercom. 'Flipping bastard, he's had his lot.'

'Well done, Ned. Do you think you really got him?'

'I don't know. Not for certain. He seemed to be going down all right, but we can only claim him as a probable. Looked like a Me 109.'

There were no more attacks from the fighter, and we kept cracking on for home. Forty-five minutes after leaving the target, the fire in the wing died right down and appeared to have gone out. We were all much happier, and I began to feel optimistic about our chances of getting back to base, or at least to England, in one piece. We were down to 4,000ft but J for Johnnie was limping along pretty well. Things could get tricky, though, if we met more light flak or another Jerry night-fighter. I called up the navigator.

'Try to check our position, Bim, will you? We've got to be careful re-crossing the enemy coast to avoid the defended areas, especially at the height we are flying at.'

'Yes, OK, skipper,' replied Bim. 'Won't be a moment. I'm just tying up Tich's hand. The silly clot got hit over the target and didn't like to say anything as we were all so busy. Anyway, he is all right and can work his set.'

'Give the bloody hero some coffee then and let me have some too. I'm parched.'

The coffee came piping hot from the Thermos flask and cheered us all up. The sneaking feeling that we might get away with it was beginning to make us feel almost light-headed. This mood was suddenly dispelled by Johnny.

'Skipper, I hate to tell you, but there seems to be smoke coming up from the bomb bays. I noticed it a short time ago.'

The silence following Johnny's announcement became impressive. The soles of my feet contracted as I thought of the full bomb load beneath them. Christ Almighty! The crew waited for me to say something.

'Johnny, for Pete's sake get a fire extinguisher and squirt the ruddy thing down through the floor wherever you can,' I said, helping him to get off the flight engineer's seat beside me.

After some interminable minutes, Johnny climbed back on to the seat and raised his thumb.

'Seems to be OK now.'

We flew on uneasily, all wrapped in one huge single thought. Were those bombs on fire?

'Enemy coast ahead.'

The tension broke as we all concentrated on watching the sky for fighters and the dim coastline for enemy defences. A searchlight suddenly came on and pointed towards us like an accusing finger. I turned towards it and dived through the beam. It began groping back to us, but by now we had crossed the coast and were over the Channel.

'Lovely grub', said Ned from his rear turret. 'That's the best thing I've seen tonight.'

We pressed on, seeing neither friend nor enemy, and made our landfall on the English coast. I felt a great love of country as we flew over those beautiful fields sleeping in the soft light.

'ETA [estimated time of arrival] base in about twenty minutes, skipper,' said Bim as he gave me a new course to steer.

Visibility was good, and we soon saw our aerodrome beacon flashing its welcome letters. I tried to call up base on the RT but found it was not working. On my instructions, Johnny got the Aldis lamp and flashed out SOS as we flew over the airfield. An answering green came back. Fine, we were cleared for landing. The flaps and undercarriage came down all right, and I turned in for the approach. However, something seemed to be wrong with the flying controls, and I could not get the aircraft into the right position. There was nothing for it but to go round again, so I belted open the throttles and pulled up the undercarriage. The duty van beside the flare path was clearly visible as we roared over.

We got on the downwind leg again, and this time everything was all right on the final approach. I flattened out over the boundary hedge and pulled the throttles right back. Just before we touched down, I realized that the starboard tyre was flat, probably from having been holed by flak over the target.

However, there could be no going around again now. I could only pray that the undercarriage did not collapse and make the aircraft end up on its belly and bomb load. Pretty tired by now, I had a tremendous desire to get back on to terra firma, whatever the risks involved.

Miraculously enough, I executed the best landing of my life, a feather-like three-pointer if ever there was one, even though I say it myself. However, as our speed began to fall off as we ran along the ground, so the flat tyre began to have the effect that a blowout has on a car. I exerted all my strength on the controls but could not prevent the Lancaster careering crazily off the flare path in a tighter and tighter turn. Cutting the magneto switches, I braked frantically until the aircraft came to a stop, giving a final shudder as though tired from its experiences. Amazingly enough, the undercarriage did not collapse.

The blood wagon, or ambulance, drove up to the aircraft in a matter of seconds and took away Tash, Tich and Johnny. The rest of us climbed wearily out and into the transport which would take us to interrogation.

'Good show, Wimpy', said Dim Wooldridge, one of our Flight commanders, who was standing there.

My knees were buckling from fatigue, but his words put new life into me. So did the tea and rum drunk during our long interrogation.

Next day, I felt terribly cold, probably because of delayed shock, and had to walk about in a heavy greatcoat. I visited poor J for Johnnie and counted 270 holes in the starboard wing alone; alas, the aircraft was declared a complete write-off.

Tich returned to the squadron very soon, but Tash and Johnny had to remain in hospital. A bit of flak had gone through Tash's neck and clipped his windpipe, but very luckily it had missed any vital parts. Johnny thought originally that he had been wounded in the leg, but in fact a bit of flak had lodged at the base of his spine. They were both in cheerful spirits when I visited them in hospital a few days later and did not take long to recover. However, I felt sure that none of us would ever forget that trip to Hamburg.

Chapter 6

More Operations

Four nights after our shaky do at Hamburg, we were detailed again for operations and dropped a 4,000lb blockbuster on Düsseldorf from 11,000ft. It was a good prang, and the fact that we did not get hit this time helped to restore my confidence. A few nights later, we went to Duisburg, and then on 8 August 1942 we did our first gardening trip. Dropping mines was called 'gardening' because the mines we carried were known as 'vegetables'. The weather was ghastly, and the whole squadron had been stood down from flying that night. Several crews prepared for a night out in Boston, while a group of us settled down to a serious game of poker after calling for a crate of beer.

The game had been in progress for a considerable time when suddenly a message was brought for my crew to report immediately for operational briefing. We were briefed to take five mines, or vegetables, and lay them in the Skagerrak near Anholt Island. Mining was often carried out when the weather was too bad for bombing, but it was unusual for a crew to be detailed for operations after the entire squadron had been stood down for the night.

The weather was absolutely lousy when we took off, and at 200ft we were already in thick cloud and rain. I think we were the only aircraft flying in weather which would keep even birds grounded. We continued on instruments and dead navigation until near the target area, where a break in the clouds enabled us to pinpoint our position. Mines had to be dropped from a fairly low height, and this time we could see what we were doing and get them in the right place. We climbed up again and flew back through solid cloud all the way to base, where we arrived five and a half hours after take-off. We had met no opposition and seen nothing except Anholt Island and the cold grey sea where we placed our vegetables. Mining was a lonely job, and you got no return for your money in the form of seeing bombs bursting on a target.

On 11 and 12 August we attacked Mainz, and three nights later, we went to Düsseldorf. On 16 August we went gardening at Salzniz, but there was cloud from 12,000ft to 600ft and, unable to find the target area, we were obliged to drop our five vegetables safe in the North Sea on the return journey. We were not allowed to drop our loads indiscriminately, but were instructed to bring them back or drop them safe in the sea if we could not locate our target.

During some of our evenings off we attended dances at the Assembly Rooms in Boston, and it was a welcome change from station life to be able to quickstep or waltz round the floor with girls dressed in civilian clothes. It was a cut and thrust business, however, because the horde of eager airmen hugely outnumbered the available partners. It was there that I had an unpleasant experience one evening with a tough aircrew member of our squadron called Sergeant Jordan. Duggie Jordan was said to have once persuaded the reluctant captain of aircraft he was flying with to press on to the target by threatening him with a fire axe. He also had the reputation of knowing beforehand exactly who was going to go missing from the squadron and was said to pack up their belongings after they had taken off and hand them over to the Padre for onward transmission to their next of kin. Duggie was always right, people said, and altogether it was rather frightening to have his clairvoyant powers around.

On this particular evening at the Assembly Rooms, it was clear to me, when Duggie lurched up to me with a pair of scissors in his hand, that he had spent far too long at the bar. At that time, some people had a habit, a very nasty one in my view, of cutting off other people's ties with scissors just below the knot. What this practice achieved or what satisfaction it gave tie-cutters was beyond my comprehension. When I saw that Duggie had designs on my tie I told him in no uncertain terms to push off smartly. For a moment, it looked as though Duggie was going to commit the serious offence of striking an officer, but fortunately, he retained, in spite of the effects of the demon ale, enough sense of discipline not to do so. Instead, he gave me a murderous look and growled, 'You will go missing within four trips.'

This prophecy left me a very worried man indeed, and I would gladly have sacrificed any ties I had if this could have made me forget it.

We did two more operations during August: one was to Frankfurt, where we dropped sixteen bundles of nickels (leaflets) in addition to our bomb load, and the other to Kassel, where we had to stick around until the end of the raid in order to do a reconnaissance of the target area for the purpose of assessing the success of the attack. In the month of September we went to Saarbrücken, Düsseldorf, Bremen, Wilhelmshaven, Essen, Munich and Wismar. The trip to Essen was a bit dicey because, as usual, the flak there was very heavy and accurate. The aircraft was hit, and so was the starboard outer engine. Most shaking of all, a piece of flak hit the rev levers while I had my hand on them. This did no damage but it certainly gave me a tremendous fright.

Tash Goodwin had now rejoined the crew and flew with us as flight engineer on our trip to Bremen on 13 September. This was his first operation since suffering the neck wound over Hamburg in July, and I could sense that he was as nervous as a cat. Every time there was a flash on the ground as a gun fired at us, poor Tash's neck jerked back, an involuntary movement which he himself probably did not notice. Every now and then, a beautiful phrase from the Liverpool docks passed his lips. A lesser man might have become a victim of that complaint known in the Forces as 'lack of moral fibre' or 'LMF', but Tash had enough guts to win the long battle he so clearly fought with his nerves that night. Our trip was trouble-free, except when the port outer airscrew got chipped over the target.

Rumours had been going round the station that the squadron might be moving, but nobody was able to obtain any definite 'gen' (information) about this before Guy Gibson gave us the news officially that the squadron would move on 1 October to Syerston, a station near Nottingham, which we would share with No. 61 (Lancaster) Squadron. I learned later that our departure from Coningsby was necessary because concrete runways were to be built there. It was rather sad to be leaving, and even sadder to see how many faces, including those of Bunny Grein and Taffy Williams, were missing from the original crowd of us who had been on the squadron in May. However, in wartime one got used to such things: posting orders came through, you packed a kitbag and moved somewhere else, often at short notice.

Moving people from one place to another was one thing, but to move an entire squadron with aircraft, ground personnel, stores and equipment required tremendous administrative management. Happily, Guy Gibson was a very capable officer with excellent organizing ability. About twenty-four years old at the time, he was a short, chunky, determined man, who was accompanied everywhere he went by his black Labrador dog. I never hit it off very well with Gibson as a person, but always had the highest admiration for him as a squadron commander.

He called the 106 aircrews together and shook us all rigid by saying that the Third Reich was to enjoy no respite from our bombing even though we were moving from one station to another. On the contrary, Butch Harris had decreed that 106 Squadron should fly on operations the very night we moved to Syerston. We had expected to have at least a day or two in which to sort ourselves out, unpack and get properly organized at the new station.

It was all a mad scramble, but we did our NFT on the one-and-a-quarter-hour flight from Coningsby to Syerston and got off the ground again that night to bomb Wismar from 5,500ft. It was a lousy return journey, because the hydraulics went unserviceable in our faithful Lancaster R5700 G for George over the target and we could not get the bomb doors closed after dropping our load. This reduced our speed and manoeuvrability. When we got home, I had to pull the emergency bottle in order to get the undercarriage and flaps down for the landing, just over seven hours after we had taken off.

Syerston was a pleasant station commanded by Group Captain Gus Walker, the international rugger player, who was one of the nicest and best stationmasters I was ever privileged to serve under. Aircrews were a fairly unruly lot to command, but he soon managed to gain our affection as well as our respect.

Members of 61 Squadron were a convivial bunch and did not seem to mind our invasion and part-occupation of their home station. Their CO was Wing Commander Slee, a tall, professorial-looking type, who had the reputation of going down to nought feet to look at the target after dropping his 4,000lb cookie from the safety height of 4,000ft, apparently ignoring the fact that he might be blown up by cookies dropped by aircraft bombing after him. Urgings to be more careful were said to make no impression on him.

We did a trip to Aachen on 5 October, and the night after that, went to Osnabrück. We ate our post-operational supper in the happy thought that we could now enjoy a week's leave. I rushed off to London with the necessary railway warrants and £10 in my pocket to spend. This was quite a large sum in those days and represented a considerable slice out of a junior officer's monthly pay.

It was on this leave that I happened to run into Paddy Davis, a friend from Brazil who was serving in the RNVR. We went off to celebrate our meeting and found our way to a downstairs bar officially called the Brasserie Universelle in Piccadilly Circus; it was known to most servicemen of the time under a much earthier name. After a couple of drinks, we started talking to a pair of rather attractive girls at the bar and soon asked them to come out with us for the evening. They refused, but invited us to join a party they were giving later that night at an address which Paddy lost no time in writing down. In due course the girls left, and we remained in pleasant meditation about the prospects of the exciting evening before us. No doubt, it would mean soft lights and sweet music in some wizard flat, we told ourselves, and we had another drink in anticipation.

When the witching hour came, we set off in a taxi to the address given. The journey took an extremely long time, and eventually we were deposited outside a block of flats miles away from our starting point. Paddy and I wondered where we were and looked at each other with dismay as we climbed an iron staircase on the outside of the building to the number of the flat we had been given. Thoughts of escape rather ungallantly took hold of us, but there could be no going back now, if only for the simple reason that we should never be able to find a taxi in these parts to take us back to the West End.

After some hesitation I rang the bell, and in a moment the door was thrown open by a large, muscular man in trousers, braces and a collarless shirt who announced himself as the local policeman. It took a little time for us to establish that the two girls we had met at the Brasserie were his daughters and that the party was in celebration of his birthday. He very kindly invited us to join the party, and we stepped inside. The lights were extremely bright, and someone was banging away on a piano, while dozens of people were making a stupendous noise. Gone were our dreams of soft lights and sweet music; this was certainly not the reception we had expected. We sang until our lungs gave out, and all the while pints of beer were thrust into our hands with agreeable if somewhat dangerous regularity. It was a magnificent party, one of the best I have ever been to. I began to feel a bit tight and wondered how on earth Paddy and I were going to get back to town. We did not have any idea where we were for a start. There was no cause to worry, however. A sympathetic red-haired woman offered to put us up for the night and, at the end of the party, took us off to her place nearby, where she made us most welcome bacon and eggs before putting us to bed.

I woke up next morning to find myself in a vast brass double bed with Paddy. Neither of us had a clue as to our whereabouts, the events of the previous evening being a bit blurred. We went downstairs and found that we were in the Bird in Hand at Shepherd's Bush, a very nice pub run by our red-haired lady. She gave us a marvellously restorative breakfast before sending us off on our return journey to the West End. I shall always remember her kindness and that of our party hosts with the deepest gratitude.

Leave was over, and it was time to return to the squadron. My crew and I got back to Syerston to find the place in turmoil. Terrific activity was going on, and the Irish labourers had been confined to camp, something unheard of in our experience. Clearly, there was a big flap on, and we longed to discover what it was all about. Finally, I got a clue. Both squadrons were to take off shortly on a daylight operation. This sounded wonderfully exciting, and we were determined not to be left out of the show. Guy Gibson finally gave me permission to go on it if I could find an aircraft, nothing being available on 106 Squadron. He suggested I try Wing Commander Slee, who agreed to lend me a spare though rather clapped-out Lancaster from 61 Squadron. With time running out fast before take-off, I rushed off to get briefed about the target. In the space of a few breathless minutes I learned that it was the Schneider works at Le Creusot, was given a route map to get there, informed about the bombing height and told to formate on two other specified aircraft towards the rear of the gaggle. The other nine Lancs from our squadron were already beginning to take off as my crew and I hared off to old S for Sugar. There was no time for a really thorough cockpit check; we got off the ground as quickly as possible and belted after the rest of the crowd, who were all flying at nought feet. While we had been on leave during the past week, the other crews had been practising loose formation flying over England at low level in daylight and had pretty well got their hands in at this rather difficult business.

We formed up with other squadrons and eventually totalled a force of ninety-four Lancasters which, to those watching us from the ground, must have been impressive in terms of quantity and noise. We crossed over Land's End and then went a long way south over the Bay of Biscay before turning in to France over the Île d'Yeu. All this time, I had been flying up and down the gaggle trying to find the other two aircraft on which we had been briefed to formate. At one stage we were even at the head of the entire formation and had extremely rude messages flashed at us with an Aldis lamp telling us to get back. It was all very shaming, but I finally managed to fall into line and take up the starboard position on the two other specified Lancasters, whose captains undoubtedly viewed us with deep misgivings as a result of my previous antics.

From the French coast we had about 200 miles to the target, and I thought that, having no escort ourselves, we might run into trouble from enemy fighters. Our gaggle roared on at low level over the countryside, and we saw people working in the fields and a man ploughing. Some waved to us while others just stood still and watched us fly past, undoubtedly surprised to see such a large force of British bombers over France in daylight. The weather was fine and there was no question of finding cloud cover if enemy fighters attacked us. However, none appeared. We had probably taken the enemy by surprise, and in any case we were a long way south of his main fighter airfields, which were placed to send aircraft up against bomber streams on their way to Germany.

It was almost dusk as we approached the target, and shortly before getting there we climbed up to our bombing height of 6,000ft. There was already a cloud of smoke rising from the Schneider works as a result of bombs dropped on it by aircraft ahead of us. However, we were hot on their heels and could still see the target clearly as we ran in. It was a successful attack, because our whole force dropped over 200 tons of bombs with precision on the target within the space of ten minutes. Someone reported afterwards that a fighter came up to have a look at the force of ninety-four Lancasters but peeled discreetly away. It was getting dark as we all climbed up and, flying independently, set course for home. It was a very long haul back to England, but there was little opposition and all our squadron aircraft made it safely. The flight had taken us nine hours and thirty-five minutes, equivalent in flying time to about two attacks on nearer targets in Happy Valley. The Le Creusot raid acted as a great fillip to us: we were scared of flying over enemy-held territory in daylight because our armament of Browning machine guns would be virtually useless against enemy fighters sitting off and pooping at us with cannon from 600 yards, yet we had now completed a long-range raid deep into enemy-held territory in broad daylight and we from the squadron had all come back to tell the tale. Details of daylight operations in our logbooks were always underlined with green ink, and I took considerable satisfaction in using this unusual colour for the first time.

Five nights later, we were briefed to attack Genoa on the eve of the great Western Desert campaign. This pleased us because Italian targets, which had been left alone for a considerable time, were reckoned to be cushy jobs and the defences not a patch on those of Germany. The main problem could come from bad weather and icing conditions during the long haul down over the Alps and back. And if you lost an engine, there was always the difficulty of getting sufficient safety height to clear those soaring, snow-covered peaks on the long journey home. If you lost two engines, then the only thing to do was to fly on to North Africa and land at some place like Casablanca. Those who had to do this found there were some compensations, as we quickly learned when they sent us messages from there saying, 'Wizard place, there's bags of sunshine and really cheap champagne.'

We had a very good bombing run and subsequently found that we had obtained a photograph of the aiming point in the dock area of Genoa. This photography business was considered very important in Bomber Command at that time. There was a synchronized system whereby a photoflash dropped out of a chute in the aircraft when we dropped our bomb load. This was timed to go off with a big flash at the moment just before our bombs hit the ground, and simultaneously a camera in the belly of the aircraft took a photograph of the place where the bombs burst. This was all very fine as long as you flew dead straight and level after releasing the bomb load for a period of some ten or fifteen seconds, but if the flak got dangerously close during this agonizing time, then your reaction was to start weaving and say, 'To hell with photography'. The camera was fixed and thus, with the aircraft standing on its beam-ends, you could be slap over the target but the photograph would show somewhere on the ground a considerable distance from the aiming point. The defences at Genoa were negligible, and we were able to fly sedately over the place until our photoflash went off and the camera took its photograph. For every aiming point photograph we were given a small certificate with a picture of a Lancaster on it, the date and name of the target and the names of the crew. Good photography showing that the bombs had fallen on or close to the aiming point helped the squadron to advance up what was called the Photographic Ladder, which was an officially-run competition in Bomber Command to show which squadrons were most accurate in their bombing.

An American sergeant pilot from our squadron called Sonny Phair put up a very good show on this Genoa trip. He lost two engines on his Lancaster but bombed the target. Instead of pressing on to North Africa, he decided to attempt the long route home along the coast since he had no hope of getting sufficient altitude to clear the Alps. It would clearly be touch and go whether he had enough fuel to make the journey. On the way back he flew over Toulon and, looking down, saw the French fleet there. As he told me afterwards, he was pessimistic at that stage about his chances of ever getting home and so, throwing caution to the winds, he circled for a considerable time, all the while sending radio messages back to England with the details and location of the warships he could see in Toulon. This was hazardous, because we were always briefed not to break radio silence except in an emergency, otherwise the enemy could pinpoint our position through messages sent by radio. With this recce report completed, Sonny Phair set course for home and eventually managed to get down at Thorney Island in the south of England with a few gallons of fuel left in his tanks. I felt strongly that he deserved a gong for this effort, but lamentably it was not forthcoming.

A few days later, on 24 October, there was another big flap, and this time we were briefed to do a daylight attack on Milan. Unfortunately, my regular aircraft was unserviceable, and instead I was given a teased-out old Lancaster pot-belly aircraft B for Beer, which was well known for its sluggishness and lack of manoeuvrability. In a pot-belly Lancaster one carried only a 4,000lb cookie or blockbuster.

A fighter escort would join us at the English coast and accompany us over the Channel to France, where the Spitfires would peel off for home. From there on we could expect cloud cover for our safety during the long flight to Milan, where we should arrive at about teatime. We received definite instructions to turn back at the French coast if we did not find the predicted cloud cover there.

All went well as far as the enemy coast, as we flew low over the sea with the comforting escort of fighters alongside us. On arrival there, the Spitfires peeled off for home, and we now had to go it alone. There was no cloud cover and visibility was excellent, the last thing we wanted. The other Lancasters had vanished entirely, and I wondered what on earth to do. After flying along for some time without seeing them I decided they must have turned for home and decided to do the same. There was no future in being a solitary Lancaster over Europe in daylight. In fact, most of them had pressed on, but we were not to know this. I turned through 180 degrees, and at this moment we went over an airfield where we could see enemy fighters taxiing out for take-off. Things were looking grim, and I therefore opened the taps and set off for a bit of cloud in the far distance. It would be suicidal to go back in clear skies, and I just wanted to get into the safety of that nice if somewhat wispy cloud, the only cover available. Just as the enemy fighters became airborne we reached our precarious hiding place but found that the thin layer of cloud stretched towards the south, not to the west where we wanted to go. It was a great temptation to stick the nose down and head for the coast, but if we did so, our Lancaster would be a sitting duck in broad daylight for ack-ack and fighters. At last, our wisp of cloud led us near the coast and I decided to make a break for it. We shot over the coastal defences, met no fighters and were soon over the Channel. The tension relaxed when the welcome sight of the English coast came up. We had got away with it but had been very lucky to do so.

We landed back at base and I felt a great sense of disappointment and frustration to see that no other aircraft were there on the dispersal pads. Clearly, we had come back when everyone else had pressed on. It was all very shaming, and I wondered unhappily whether members of the squadron would think, though they would never say it, that I had turned back through cowardice. I cheered up a little when it was discovered after landing that the oil system, hydraulics and practically everything else in the aircraft had gone unserviceable. Oil and glycol were pouring out of it.

The engineering officer came up and said, 'Thank Heavens you came back, Wimpy, because this old crate would never have got to the target and back in the state it's in.'

Three of us had turned back from the operation, and the other two were shot down. Later, the squadron crews came back jubilant from a successful daylight attack on Milan, where they had met little opposition and obviously shaken the Italians rigid.

Soon afterwards, we were due for another night bombing raid, and I had an extremely heavy cold. One was not supposed to fly in such a state because damage could then be caused to ears at altitude. I was afraid of losing the use of my only good ear and therefore reported to our medico, Doctor Arnold by name. All I wanted was for him to check my serviceable ear and ban me from flying that night because of my heavy cold. However, he was a thorough doctor and, despite my protests and evasions, insisting on seeing my duff ear as well. He took one look and sent me off to RAF Hospital, Cosford, near Wolverhampton. I packed my things for the journey with an ill grace and wondered whether I should ever get back to the squadron again. Crews were usually given a rest after completing a first operational tour of thirty trips before coming back to do a second lot, and here I was going off to hospital with only twenty-seven trips to my credit.

After saying goodbye to my crew I went by transport into Nottingham and there discovered that there was a delay of some two hours before the train left for Worcestershire. Feeling thoroughly browned off, I repaired to the upstairs bar of the Black Boy, one of the squadron's favourite haunts, and decided to drown my sorrows in the 106 Special. This drink had been devised after exhaustive research by an Australian from our squadron called Johnny Coates, who wanted to invent something original, and the barmaids in the Black Boy were well experienced in the art of preparing it. The form was to put a dash of orange bitters in a tumbler, add a tot of orange Curaçao and a tot of whisky, and fill up with ginger ale and ice. The result tasted very pleasant and apparently harmless, but only those familiar with the concoction knew from experience that nobody could drink more than six 106 Specials without being overtaken by a sort of creeping paralysis of the locomotor system, although the brain remained as clear as a bell. Never having had more than two of them before, I now downed six of the 106 Specials and had an awful train journey afterwards into Worcestershire, during which I felt at every moment that the hospital at Cosford was probably the best place for me. I checked in there and retired thankfully to a bed in quite a large ward.

Cosford consisted of a group of Nissen huts isolated in the countryside, but the standard of comfort and medical attention was high in spite of wartime conditions. The nurses were sweet and charming and cheered us all up by saying that the doctors there usually reckoned to be able to save anyone who reached Cosford alive. We were woken up every morning at some ungodly hour and often had to stand by our beds for inspection by the Matron, an impressive lady who really saw to it that everything was shipshape and Bristol fashion and, if it wasn't, then by God you were for the high jump. She was a woman of rare breed and quality.

Most of the patients in my ward were walking cases like myself, and every day we reported to our respective doctors for treatment. My quack was an Australian, an extremely nice man, who tried out some extract of maggots on my bad ear. An air gunner in our ward was being treated for a stomach ulcer, but the chap we really felt sorry for was a cheerful character who constantly had his lung deflated by means of a long needle, the sight of which was enough to make me turn my head away. I remember long conversations with another patient called Squadron Leader Chetle, who had been ADC to the Viceroy of India. Hospital life was a period of frustration and intense boredom, and we tried to while away the time by reading, talking or making model aeroplanes.

We were allowed out very little, but once I managed to visit Boscobel, the charming country house where Charles II hid in the oak tree. This was of special interest to me because my family is descended from the Pendrell brothers, who hid him in that tree.

The local pub was miles away, and any hopes of sinking some quiet pints there in the evening were cancelled out by the fact that we were supposed to be back in our wards by 6.00 pm. Nevertheless, several of us broke the rules by going there and subsequently gaining entry to the hospital by unofficial means well after the witching hour. During one of these escapades, I met a Dutch friend for whom I had worked in Brazil before the war. I think he was serving in the Princess Irene regiment.

'Come and dine in our regimental Mess', he said. 'And then we can talk about old times.'

I learned that it would be necessary to travel about two stations from Cosford by train to get there but accepted the invitation to dine in the Mess on a particular evening. I sneaked out of Cosford successfully and eventually arrived at the Dutch Mess. The trouble was that their hospitality was apparently limitless. My Dutch friend introduced me to each of his brother officers as they came in to the Mess, and every one of them insisted on giving me a drink. My counting became shaky, but I think there must have been eighteen of them. After this, we had a marvellous dinner of East Indian food, accompanied by red-hot sauces. At the end of the evening, I was placed in a large Austin motorcar and driven off to the railway station in time to catch the last train back to Cosford. After an uneasy journey, I arrived back at the hospital in a very cheerful state and disgraced myself by uprooting an 'Entry Forbidden' sign and planting it at the entrance to the nurses' sleeping quarters. This was a silly schoolboy antic, but it expressed all my frustration at being in hospital instead of on operational flying. My return at an illegal hour had not been accomplished without considerable noise, and I realized that I should catch a packet next day from the Matron and possibly be subjected to all sorts of restrictions in the future.

Things turned out unexpectedly from my point of view. RAF Hospital Cosford obviously considered that I was well enough to go elsewhere, because on the following morning I was told to report in London for a medical. This took place on Christmas Eve with a RAF specialist called Dr Simpson, a man who knew his stuff completely.

'Officially you are not fit to fly', he said, 'but I see you did quite a bit of flying before going to hospital. Do you want to go back on operations?'

'Yes', I said.

'Right', he replied. 'I shouldn't do it but I'll pass you A1B.'

Hardly believing my good luck, I returned to 106 Squadron at Syerston and was delighted to find my crew still there. I took an extremely good view of Guy Gibson for having retained them for me during the two months of hospital; he would have been fully justified in crewing them up with another captain or using them to fill gaps.

On 28 December I did some local flying with my crew in a Lancaster to get my hand in again and that night went off again to do circuits and bumps, taking with me three aircrew members who were spare bodies on the squadron. The weather was dreadful, and we got lost almost immediately. We flew round and round in low cloud looking for either base or the satellite airfield. This was not the night to practise circuits and bumps, I thought, peering down through the murk and seeing nothing.

'You're down to 80ft, skipper' said one of the crew warningly, his eyes glued to the altimeter.

Stiffen the crows! Two months off flying had certainly made me lose my touch. Finally, we picked up the beacon and I made a shaky approach to Syerston, the other crew members obviously feeling as jittery as I was. One engine cut, and things began to look even worse. At last, we saw the flare path and I came in for the landing, praying hard. On the final approach, another engine cut out but we got in safely, though shaken mightily. Back in the Mess, other pilots ticked me off good-humouredly for low flying over the airfield, but I think they realized the agony I had gone through trying to get down in one piece.

My first trip after returning to the squadron was on 3 January 1943, and the target was our old enemy, Essen. We were briefed that there would be only fourteen aircraft on the target and that a new technique called Wanganui would be used. This meant that the Pathfinders would drop special flares over the target and we would aim our bombs at those flares in the air while we flew on a specified heading. The Pathfinders could locate the target by means of special equipment and drop their aiming flares accurately, and we would be able to hit our objective even though it was obscured by cloud. This was a revolutionary idea, and we wondered how the system would work. Cloud over the target was our bugbear, and this new Wanganui thing, if successful, would open up entirely new possibilities. We were now briefed to fly much higher and, instead of bombing from 12,000ft or 15,000ft, we went in this time at 20,300ft. The extra height did not save us from the heavy flak, which went up to 30,000ft or 40,000ft and was as accurate as ever over Essen. There was cloud when we got there, but we had no trouble in seeing the special flares and aiming our load at them in the prescribed manner. We weaved out of the target area without getting hit and headed for home and post-operational bacon and egg. This raid was apparently successful, and its impact on the Germans must have been considerable, since they would now realize that we had a technique for bombing a target through cloud.

On 8 December something terrible happened at Syerston. There was an op on that night, but my crew had been given the evening off. Suddenly the door of the Mess anteroom shook as though from the effect of a faraway explosion. We learned afterwards that a 4,000lb cookie had fallen out of the bomb doors of a Lancaster as it was being bombed up. Gus Walker had rushed to the aircraft with a crash crew and together they started to roll the cookie away to get it clear of the aircraft, but as they were doing so, it exploded. Windows were blown out in Newark seven miles away, but nobody in the crash crew right beside the cookie was killed, although many were severely injured. Gus Walker had his arm blown off and was found wandering around the airfield in a dazed condition. A man of great courage, he returned about two months later to take over command of the station again.

Guy Gibson now gave Sonny Phair and me a real operational pasting by making us do four trips in five nights to Happy Valley, which was pushing it a bit. Other crews from the squadron were available, but we were the only two who were put on to fly during those nights. On 8 January 1943 we went to Duisburg, where the flak was extremely hot. The aircraft was hit, the port outer engine was put out of action, and we had to return on three. The next night, we went to Essen and got some flak through the windscreen. The wind coming in at way-below-zero temperatures soon froze my face. Two nights after that, it was Essen again, and the night after that, Essen once more. We were really tired by this time, and depressed, because on 13/14 January Sonny Phair failed to return. I felt we had been pushed too far, and others thought the same. One friend told me that there could well have been a mutiny on the station had my crew been put on to fly yet again.

Three nights later, my crew and I had an easy trip to Berlin lasting eight hours and forty minutes, carrying an 8,000lb cookie, which was possibly the first one to be dropped on the place. The next night, we took another 8,000lber to Berlin, and our photograph taken on the bombing run showed the JU 88 engine factory three miles south-south-west of Tempelhof. The flak was much heavier this time and got frighteningly close to us. Even worse was the return journey, because we had to fly through great masses of seemingly impenetrable dirty black cloud which caused the aircraft to ice up, something which could be even more frightening than enemy defences. You climbed for safety, but on the way the aircraft began icing up and getting heavier and heavier on the controls, while the performance fell off. Then big lumps of ice started to break off and knock holes in the fuselage. Often this was coupled with St Elmo's fire, which was an eerie blue light forming round the propellers and even coming out of your hands. Flashes of lightning helped to create the atmosphere of some strange, evil world into which we had trespassed and which was trying its best to destroy us. Never were stars so comforting to see as when you began to catch a glimpse of them through the thinning, uppermost layers of the cloud; this meant that you had almost won the battle to get above it. Once on top, there was the peace of clear skies and a dramatic panorama of cloud canyons, mountains and plains, lit by an occasional flash as though the Devil himself were striking gigantic matches in the Hades below. One's imagination could run riot in these conditions. The weather was bad when we got back to England, and we were diverted to Marham.

The fact that nobody else from the squadron had flown on operations while Sonny Phair and I had been put on so often, coupled with his loss, made me feel resentful, and one day I vented my spleen on the Australian Dave Shannon, who was in our Flight.

'Why aren't you and the other fellows from this squadron flying on operations for a change instead of leaving it all to us?' I asked him testily.

'Ah, we are being reserved for special targets', he replied.

'No doubt nice easy Italian ones', I said unkindly.

I have never really understood why Guy Gibson treated Sonny Phair and myself as so much cannon fodder during that period, or why other crews, with perfectly serviceable aircraft, spent night after night on the ground while we were 'juggling with Jesus' over Happy Valley. I later wondered if Gibson already knew then that he would soon be taken off regular operations in order to begin training 617 Squadron for the brilliant dams raid and was saving crews captained by Dave Shannon, Hoppy Hopgood and others from 106 for this great operation. If this was so, then I believe that the Lone Ranger-type efforts of Sonny Phair and myself were worthwhile. However, at the time I took a dim view of the way we had been treated, so much so that when a notice appeared on our Squadron board calling for volunteers to join the Pathfinders it gave me considerable food for thought. A change might be a good thing, and in any case, it would be interesting to fly ahead of the main force and drop markers to light the target. My crew felt the same way about it.

A few days later, we did an NFT, and after a perfectly normal and respectable landing I was summoned immediately to Gibson's office.

'That was a bloody awful landing you've just done', he said.

'I think it was rather a good landing, sir', I replied with righteous indignation, for I had been quite pleased with it.

'Well, the landing may have been all right, but you approached very high.'

'My approach was perfectly normal, sir.'

This conversation was beginning to puzzle me. If there had been anything out of the ordinary about my approach and landing, then I should have been ready to admit it. However, this was a frontal attack based on groundless accusations.

'Well, all right, but you used your brakes very violently after touching down.'

I had hardly used my brakes after landing but had let the Lancaster roll along to the end of the runway. I thought of Sonny Phair, and my temper began to rise.

'Sir, I've seen the notice on the board calling for volunteers to join the Pathfinders, and my crew and I wish to apply.'

Gibson looked at me thoughtfully. 'They only want the best crews and so I shouldn't think you stand a chance.' He then added quite charmingly, 'But I'll do my best for you.'

Our swansong operation with 106 Squadron was to Hamburg on 30 January 1943. I had a nasty feeling about the place by virtue of our experience there, but in the event everything went well and it was not too bad a trip.

Gibson was as good as his word, because the acceptance of my application to join the Pathfinders now came through, and as a result, my crew and I were transferred on 7 February 1943 to 83 Squadron at RAF Wyton in Huntingdonshire. It was a wrench to leave the squadron on which we had served for nearly a year, and later on we felt a bit done out of it when many of our chums from 106 were transferred to the new 617 Squadron under Gibson's command to carry out the dams raid. However, at that time we had no inkling that this was afoot.

Bim Bone, Tich Webster, Ned Needham and Nobby Naylor were no longer with us, and the crew members who accompanied me to RAF Wyton were Vin Harley, Tash Goodwin and Sergeant Hicks, a rear gunner who had already done seven trips with us on 106 Squadron. Dusty Hicks was a slim, quiet, good-looking American, who had, I think, been a golf professional in Syracuse. Imperturbable and a man of few words, Dusty was a thoroughly good type to have around anywhere at any time. The United States Air Force had tried to woo him away with offers of a commission as Second Lieutenant and what for us was fabulous pay, but Dusty resisted their advances in order to remain in the RAF. Vin Harley, Tash Goodwin and Dusty Hicks stuck with me right to the end of my second tour of operations and they were the best bunch of crew members that any captain of aircraft could possibly find

One became attached to particular aircraft, and it had therefore been sad to leave 106 Squadron Lancaster G for George, which had carried us on sixteen operational trips. Each trip was represented by a small bomb painted on the port side of the fuselage, just forward of the cockpit. G for George also bore an emblem which nearly caused an international incident. Guy Gibson had decided that each aircraft on the squadron should have an emblem, together with a name of the pilot's choice prefixed by the word Admiral. I never understood the reason for this nautical flavor, but there it was. I cannot recall that such inspiring names as Drake or Nelson were chosen, and indeed some of them were enough to make a maiden blush. Tich Webster, our wireless operator, painted a very artistic Walt Disney Dumbo carrying a bomb as our G for George crest, and Walt Disney himself could not have found fault with the result.

'What name shall I paint on, skipper?' asked Tich, ready with his paintbrush to complete the job.

'I'm damned if I can think of anything', I replied. 'This had better be decided by the whole crew.'

'What about something rude in Portuguese from Brazil?' suggested Tash.

'Yes, let's have that', said the rest of the crew.

'OK, then', I replied. 'Paint on "Admiral *Filho da Puta*".'

This at its best can be translated as 'son of a bitch'.

We rather liked the results of Tich's handiwork and certainly had no idea that any political implications might ensue. Not long afterwards, a photographer from the magazine *Illustrated* turned up at the station to photograph squadron aircraft. He apparently rejected some of the English names as being unsuitable, and then, while casting about, his eye lit on G for George; he thought the foreign wording rather interesting, though he did not understand its meaning. Being away on leave at the time, I was unable to stop him taking a photograph of our emblem, which subsequently appeared in *Illustrated*. I was told afterwards that a copy of the magazine was shown indignantly to Getulio Vargas, then President of Brazil, who, far from being shocked, was much amused by our emblem and asked for further copies of the magazine. Only in 1944 did I hear that the Germans had used the photograph for propaganda purposes by superimposing the Portuguese coat of arms on the Dumbo and claiming that this was how British bomber pilots desecrated the arms of Portugal. I never did hear the full story but understood that some brilliant fellow in the Air Ministry managed to counter the German attack by saying that the name '*Filho da Puta*' given to G for George was in fact in honour of a racehorse of this name which won the Great St Leger in 1815 (quite true, it was that a horse of this name won that race). The print of this horse is much sought after by people connected with South America, and I myself have had one for many years as a remembrance of the saga of the emblem on our Lancaster G for George.

Chapter 7

Pathfinders

We soon settled down at RAF Wyton and found it a most congenial station. In addition to the 83 Squadron Lancasters we had a squadron of Mosquitoes, which were often engaged on diversionary raids. We also had based with us a flight of Mosquitoes doing Met or weather reconnaissance over Europe, the code name for these flights being 'Pampa'. These splendid aircraft, the Mozzies, had no armament but relied for safety on speed and the great height at which they could fly. They were made of wood, and so any damage to them could usually be repaired by a carpenter. Even though it was a comparatively small aeroplane, with a crew of only two, the Mosquito could carry a 4,000lb blockbuster, something the Flying Fortress of that time could not do. It was undoubtedly one of the finest aircraft ever produced, and its value to us in the air war was inestimable.

My crew now acquired a navigator called Tommy Blair, a great character who had already completed many operations. Tommy was a beefy, lovable, extrovert type from Durham who didn't really care a damn for anybody. He was the very devil on a party and had no knuckles left on his right hand as a result of hitting people while under the influence. However, nobody seemed to hold it against Tommy. He enjoyed singing, and long-suffering brother officers in the Mess were soon subjected to our joint rendering of 'Kalamazoo', which had become the crew song. Tommy was not one of your brilliant, egg-headed navigators but he was one who got you to the target on time and back again to base in an efficient manner. He had a 'couldn't care less' attitude to the dangers of operational flying and to the problems of life in general. The floppy cap without stiffeners that he wore symbolized his attitude to any form of authoritarian bull.

We now had a wireless operator called Earl Reid, a Canadian Flight Lieutenant who was a first-class type, and a gunner called Connor to complete the crew. Together with Vin Harley, Tash Goodwin and Dusty Hicks, we were all quite experienced on operations, which was a requirement for crews joining the Pathfinders. An extra though unofficial member of our crew was Sammy, Tommy's cocker spaniel, who always flew with us and who had already chalked up quite a number of operations with Tommy in previous days. Sammy used to lie under the navigator's table next to his master's feet and was always as good as gold, whether it was an operational flight on a bombing raid or just local flying. No amount of weaving over the target disturbed him, and he took no notice of the flak whatsoever. Sammy knew infallibly when we were coming in to land by the sound of the increased revs and the airscrews going into fine pitch. He then got to his feet and sometimes put his front paws up on the side of the fuselage, trying to have a look through the Perspex window. He possibly had more operational flying hours to his credit than any other dog in the world. Sammy would get the chop if we were shot down, but even so it was, in my view, kinder to have him with us than to leave him behind at the station. I had seen bewildered dogs waiting at aircraft dispersal points for their masters who were not going to return from a raid. One resolutely refused to budge for weeks, and the ground crew took food and water to the place where it lay day and night waiting hopefully for its master's aircraft to return.

We had joined B Flight, commanded by Squadron Leader Cook, and were put on operations within a week of our arrival at Wyton. On 13 February 1943 we bombed the submarine pens at Lorient and had a nice easy trip lasting no more than four hours and thirty minutes. The powers that be were keen at this time that we should attack the submarine pens at places like Lorient and St Nazaire, but I don't think that even a direct hit with a 4,000lb cookie would have made much impression on their immensely thick concrete construction; and there was the danger of causing casualties among the French civilian population. However, it was not for us to question the wisdom of target selections; our job was to carry out the orders we received at briefing to the best of our ability.

On the following night we did a long trip to Spezia, the Italian port, and our total force on the target this time consisted of only four bombers. It was a successful prang, and we brought back a photograph of the aiming point.

During the next fortnight we did trips to Lorient, Wilhemshaven, Bremen and Cologne. On 28 February we went to St Nazaire, which was considered to be an easy target from the point of view of enemy defences. Nevertheless, I somehow managed to get coned in both searchlights and have a shaky do, with the result that we got five flak holes in the aircraft. Afterwards in the Mess everybody thought it terribly funny that we should have had this trouble over a target that was considered to be a piece of cake, but I could not share in the amusement.

On evenings off we often went to the George at Huntingdon, where mine host Johnny, the kindliest of men, treated us like a father, mother and brother. When the cry of 'Time, gentlemen, please' went up he usually signalled to us to go into another room, and then, when the pub doors had been locked, produced more beer. Another favourite of ours was the Pike and Eel at St Ives, a charming pub by the river. One evening, Tommy and I were having a drink there and talking to a Flight Lieutenant from our squadron whose name I cannot recall. A night or two later, the Flight Lieutenant and his crew went missing on operations. About a month afterwards, Tommy and I walked into the bar of the Pike and Eel, and there was our Flight Lieutenant sitting in exactly the same place at the corner of the bar where he had been at our last meeting. For one wild moment I thought it must be his ghost.

'What the hell are you doing here?' we asked. 'You were supposed to have gone missing.'

'I did', he replied, 'but now I'm back.'

After being shot down he had got over the Pyrenees into Spain, presumably with the help of an escape organization, and was there put into a Spanish prison, where he had all his head shaved. Somebody then extricated him and sent him back to England. He had completed an extraordinarily quick round trip. For obvious reasons, he was not to be drawn about the actual details of his escape, since careless talk could prejudice the safety of others.

As operational aircrew we had to be extremely careful about security and, to hammer this point home, there were notices everywhere saying, 'Careless talk costs lives' or urging us to 'Be like Dad, keep Mum'. As members of the Pathfinder Force we had to be particularly careful, because we were using special equipment and techniques, any details of which could be of great value to the enemy. An officer once gave us a lecture about some special equipment we were to use and held up a piece from it.

'This bit is called the so-and-so', he said, 'but you must never ever mention that name and if you hear anyone doing so then you must report him immediately to higher authority.'

We thought it unnecessary for him to have mentioned the unmentionable name.

After doing the requisite number of trips as a marker of targets, we were awarded the Pathfinder Force Badge, a gold eagle fixed by two screws to the top of our left breast pockets on uniform and battledress. It had to be removed before operations, otherwise an enemy interrogating officer would see it and give us a thorough going over; but we wore the badge all the time in England and were thus easily identifiable as members of the Pathfinder Force. There were undoubtedly those working for the enemy who tried to extract information from operational aircrew, but on the whole, our security was reasonably good. It was a question of refusing to be provoked or resisting the temptation to 'shoot a line'. However, it was not always easy to cancel dates with girlfriends with evasive statements like, 'Sorry, I'm on duty tonight', when one felt like saying, 'The evening's off because I shall be flying over bloody Berlin tonight.'

I once had an odd experience while travelling by train to London. My compartment was shared by a foreign gentleman in civilian clothes who looked just like a German spy. He eyed my uniform and, after a long pause, said in guttural accents, 'From what base are you coming?'

'Oh, from the cold, cold north', I replied airily, on the principle that anywhere north of the Thames was liable to be cold.

He tried several other questions on me and then, after another long pause, said with a knowing look in his eye, 'Perhaps you are coming via Murmansk, yes?'

The only thing to do in such cases was to choke off the questioner by saying that you were not permitted to give any information about the location or nature of your unit.

Operations continued, and we were now achieving saturation by concentrating a large number of bombers on to a target in a short time, something that required considerable organization and good timing. We in the Pathfinders carried, in addition to our normal bomb loads, such special devices as Target Indicator Greens or Pink Pansies, with which to mark the aiming point for the main force, and we had a permissible leeway of no more than sixty seconds on either side of our specified bombing time, not much on an outward journey of perhaps three or four hours. If we were delayed for any reason then we were forbidden to drop our markers at the wrong time but had to join the main force and drop our bomb loads when they went in to the attack. During the first week of March we went to Berlin, Hamburg, Essen and Nuremberg. Tommy was not with us for the Nuremberg trip, and his place was taken by an officer who had a very high reputation as a skilled navigator. All went well until the return journey, when I became increasingly worried about our position. We appeared to be over the edge of a city, and this was not right. The navigator had been taking star shots from the astrodome and was now working busily with his maps and compasses.

'Where do you think we are?' I asked.

'Not to worry, skipper', he replied confidently. 'We should be absolutely bang on track.'

'Well, I'm damned sure we're bang over the centre of Gay Paree, and we're going to get the hell out of here', I replied, turning sharply on to another course.

The navigator was rather crestfallen to discover that we were in fact seventy miles off track. So much for astro-navigation, I thought; let's stick to dead reckoning and the visual identification of landmarks.

On 9 March we had a shaky do over Munich after being badly coned by searchlights and shot at really heavily. I invited Tommy to come out from behind his navigator's curtain to see the fun, and at that moment we began getting hit by flak. A small piece hit Tommy on the arm, and for days he was rubbing the place with a toothbrush in order to show the angry mark to admiring friends. Getting coned by searchlights over a heavily-defended target was no joke, however. You felt like a trapped bird as, weaving desperately about, you tried to get out of the terrible light shone up by those crouching beasts, which pursued their prey so relentlessly. It was like being on stage at the Windmill Theatre with all the spotlights on and the audience shooting at you. The flak guns concentrated on you and pumped up everything they had, while you sweated and swore and flung the aircraft about in frantic manoeuvres which would probably have made the designer's hair stand on end. Moreover, if the flak suddenly stopped, then you knew that the fighters were closing in, and your tummy contracted even more in expectation of a sudden blasting by cannon shells. We finally got out of Munich into glorious darkness and found ourselves flying at about 6,000ft. The homeward trip was uneventful, and over the Channel we restored ourselves with pineapple juice, coffee and a cigarette.

Two nights later, we went to Stuttgart, and the night after that to Essen where, as usual, we got everything thrown at us including the kitchen stove. For a few days after this we were on training flights, and it was not until 22 March that we went on operations again, this time to St Nazaire.

We were now due for a week's leave, and Tommy and I went straight off to London, where we seemed to spend most of our time in the Coconut Grove. We were always very well looked after by Edmundo Ros and the other band playing there, and they used to take us backstage and feed us bacon and eggs and whisky. We were also fond of a sixteen-year-old singer there called June, who was heavily chaperoned by her mother at all times, certainly while we were around. In addition, there was a very charming cigarette girl called Molly, who always welcomed us with a smile and plenty of backchat. They were a really nice lot at the Coconut Grove.

During leaves in London I often met Mac, or MacLachlan, the one-armed fighter pilot who distinguished himself in the famous air battles over Malta. We became friends at Wyton, where he used to come and do fighter affiliation with us; this meant that he turned up in his fighter at an agreed time and made simulated air-to-air attacks on a Lancaster detailed for this exercise. What we learned from this would be very useful in any combats with Jerry fighters over Europe. The tremendous slipstream from a weaving four-engined bomber was a great defence against fighters coming in from astern, because the turbulence threw them all over the place and was sometimes enough to turn them over on their backs. This manoeuvre worked successfully with most fighter pilots practising fighter affiliation with us, but not with Mac. Whatever you did, he was always right there behind within shooting distance, and I was glad that he was a friend and not an enemy. He flew really beautifully. One day, he asked me whether he could fly my Lancaster and, with some trepidation, I agreed. Even with one arm, he flew it wonderfully well, although I naturally had to help with the opening of the throttles.

At a dinner party many years after the war in Rio de Janeiro I was talking to a fellow guest named Luigi who, as a member of the Italian Air Force, had flown on sorties against Malta.

'Did you know Mac?' was his first question on learning that I had served in the RAF.

'Yes, we were good friends,' I replied. 'But where did you meet him?'

The whole story then came out. Luigi had been shot down by Mac over Malta and badly damaged in the process. He was put into hospital and underwent many operations. He was coming round from one of them when he noticed another bed in his room. It was occupied by Mac, who had himself been shot down, losing his arm. Mac and Luigi became firm friends, and these two enemies clearly felt a great deal of affection for each other. They always refused to go down to the air-raid shelter when an attack on Malta was taking place, and so a nurse in a tin hat used to sit with them while the raid lasted.

'Do you know what happened to Mac?' asked Luigi. 'I would love to get in touch with him again.'

'No, we lost contact in 1943 when the RAF sent me on a trip overseas. However, Air Ministry Records should be able to give us some details. I'll write to them and let you know as soon as their reply comes back.'

In due course, a very sympathetically-written letter arrived from the Air Ministry saying that Mac had been killed over France and that members of the Resistance had placed flowers on his grave. I passed the unwelcome news on to Luigi, whose face pictured the dismay and sadness he felt at hearing it.

We returned to Wyton after leave and on 8 April went on operations to Duisburg. On this night, an angry Tash Goodwin had to give up his place in the crew to a newly-arrived Australian captain called Sergeant King, whom I had been briefed to take on this operation as second pilot. The old system of carrying a second dickey as a regular crew member had been discontinued, no doubt because it had proved too expensive, and flight engineers had taken their places. However, new captains could not be thrust over enemy territory without being given a couple of trips as second pilot in order to gain experience. We had a remarkably easy trip to Duisburg, which appeared to me to make Sergeant King a little overconfident.

'Trips are not usually so easy', I told him. 'For Pete's sake make sure you weave, not only to avoid the flak but to enable your gunners to get a good look round for any enemy fighters coming in.'

He did not seem to be very impressed by this advice. Shortly afterwards, Sergeant King, flying with his own crew, was shot down by a fighter which they apparently never saw. The story we heard afterwards was as follows. The fighter crept up and squirted cannon shells into the Lancaster, which blew up in the air. The first thing Sergeant King knew was that he was floating down on his parachute. He had a nasty wound in his arm from a cannon shell. After hitting the ground, he started walking but was quickly picked up by a German army patrol. King had thrust a hand into his battledress blouse in order to support his wounded arm, and the Germans, thinking he was trying to draw a gun, prodded him with their bayonets. They insisted he must be a spy because he was alone. If he had come out of a shot down British bomber, then where had the other members of the crew got to? Thinking him a dangerous man, the military handed King over to the Gestapo, who interrogated him endlessly. He had still received no medical attention at all. The questioning went on and on. If he claimed to be a British bomber pilot, then what had become of the other crew members? Sergeant King could only reply that he must have been the sole survivor when the aircraft blew up. Eventually, he was put in a cell, where the temperature varied between blazing hot and icy cold. The shock of these changes probably saved him from passing out altogether, as he had lost a lot of blood. Finally, he was placed in hospital for treatment, which he badly needed, and even there the orderlies could not refrain from using mental torture on him. They would come to his bedside in the morning and say, 'Well, you will be having your arm off this afternoon.' He sweated it out for hours, but nobody came to wheel him away to the operating theatre. This happened more than once. He never did have his arm off, but in the end was returned in poor physical shape to England under a prisoner of war exchange. This was the story that filtered through to us eventually and it provoked a feeling of cold rage. I never saw Sergeant King again and was therefore unable to get the full details from him personally.

Two nights after Duisburg, we went to Frankfurt, the city where my future father-in-law had served as HM Consul General for seven years up to the outbreak of war. On departure he was obliged to leave his furniture behind, and it was subsequently all destroyed during attacks by the RAF, something he has constantly though good-humouredly blamed me for personally. What rankled with him most was the destruction of his grand piano, but I always replied that, if I were the culprit who blew up his piano, then this would be a great tribute to the accuracy of my bombing.

The Commanding Officer of our squadron was now Wing Commander James Gillman, a rather military-looking type with a toothbrush moustache who had announced his intention of doing one operational trip with every crew on the squadron. This was a laudable idea, but we liked James Gillman and felt that his declared policy of crew chop and change on operations would end in the chop for him. Unfortunately, we were right, as he was killed on 5 May 1943 on an op to Dortmund.

On 13 April we were briefed to attack some battleships in Spezia, and Wing Commander Gillman decided to fly as my second pilot, which meant that Tash Goodwin had to stand down. We also took as an extra bod Wing Commander MacGown, who was the Group eye specialist and expert on night vision. Crews did not usually like taking extra bodies on operations because of space and oxygen supply considerations, but in the case of Doc MacGown we would willingly have done without our own oxygen in order to have him along. He was one of the nicest men I have ever met, tall, thin, grey-haired, a true Scot with the aquiline features of a Regency aristocrat. The complete gentleman and a wonderful friend, Doc had flown in the First World War and always said he was completing his second tour of operations in this one.

There were very few aircraft on Spezia that night. We dropped flares over the target area and did our first run-in. The weather was all right, the defences were nothing to worry about and our bombing run was bang on. However, we simply could not find the battleships. I did six runs over the target at 6,000ft, but we were still unable to see the objective. On the final run, Wing Commander Gillman said, 'Let's bomb and get the hell out of here.' We dropped our bombs in the scheduled area and got home nine hours after we had taken off. The photographs showed that we had sunk not a battleship, but a destroyer, and at least this was some return for a long trip.

The next night, we bombed Stuttgart, and this was a successful and trouble-free raid as far as we were concerned. Dusty Hicks could not fly that night, and his place in the rear turret was taken by a remarkable character called Flying Officer Watkins, generally known as Watty, who was a dashing, Latin-looking type with a thin black moustache. I could visualize Watty, cigarette hanging from upper lip below a Mexican sombrero, playing a languorous guitar or dancing a gay señorita off her feet to the strains of 'La Comparsita'. Watty was alleged to have been cashiered in the past, people muttered darkly, but these remarks did not worry me because I liked him and found him to be an efficient member of aircrew as a gunner. However, there was one terrible night in the Mess when Watty, high as a kite, found the Station Commander's cap sitting on the anteroom table and proceeded to treat it in a way that does not bear description. I washed the hat as well as I could and placed it on the table again next to the Station Commander's stick. Next morning, the Station Commander came out after breakfast, picked up the cap and put it on his head. Alas, it had shrunk to dwarf-like size and perched ridiculously on top of his head. From my discreet observation point I saw him throw the cap down in a rage and stamp off to his office.

Shortly afterwards, Watty, fearful of the disciplinary action which was bound to follow, came twittering to me in the Flight Office and asked what he should do. The trouble was that the station commander was a most unpopular man. A stickler for unnecessary forms of discipline, he had demanded nine arrests a day on the squadron as a matter of routine. This was a nonsensical requirement and, in order to satisfy it, the point was reached where Leading Aircraftsmen were arrested for not standing to attention when talking to Corporals; others had been arrested outside the camp for not walking in step together. Believing that the cap episode would bring stiff reprisals, I advised Watty to go to the Commanding Officer and make a clean breast of the whole ghastly incident. He paled slightly but trotted off obediently, leaving me wondering whether we should ever see him again.

To my astonishment a jubilant Watty was back again within an hour. The CO had accepted his explanation most readily and thanked him for coming to him. He had said that it was a great relief to him to hear that it was an individual escapade, because he had feared it might be a combined squadron gesture against him for, he added rather sadly, he knew he was unpopular with us. Watty got off scot-free. I rather took my hat off to the CO for his attitude, although this is perhaps not a suitable expression in the circumstances. He was soon transferred, and we got a more tolerant station commander in his place.

The chief of the Pathfinder Force was Air Vice-Marshal Don Bennett, and he and his very charming wife lived in married quarters on the station at RAF Wyton. I liked him and always had the highest admiration for the way in which he ran the force under his command and carried on the bombing effort with ruthlessness, energy and determination. Neither Butch Harris nor Don Bennett received proper public recognition afterwards for their invaluable services during the Second World War, but at the time they both certainly won loyalty, respect and an odd kind of affection from the bomber crews who served them. We never queried their decisions, though we often moaned about them, because we had complete confidence in them. I think England was lucky to have men of that calibre at the top of their particular trees at that particular time. Don Bennett was an aviation expert who brought his penetrating mind to bear on the problems of bombing Germany with relentlessness, dedication and devastating efficiency. He knew what he wanted and did not allow red tape to stand in his way. If we needed a particular piece of equipment, then Don Bennett had no hesitation in driving his car at enormous speed to Air Ministry stores in London and removing the piece required from the shelves, while horrified storekeepers protested unsuccessfully that he should indent in writing. Through his personal efforts we got what we required in double quick time and were spared long weeks of paper warfare, something which could have seriously hampered our bomber offensive. Don Bennett had very heavy policy, planning and administrative responsibilities but he still managed to find time now and then to fly on operations with PFF crews. One day, we were briefed that the AOC would be flying with us that night, and special equipment was loaded into our aircraft.

'What the hell is all that gubbins for?' I asked the ground crew.

'Oh, the AOC will use it for recording his impression of the raid', they replied.

My crew and I were flattered at the prospect of taking the AOC with us but felt nervous in case we should drop some clanger.

'Christ,' said Tommy, 'that man knows more about navigation than all of us navigators on the squadron put together. He even wrote a book about it.'

'That's all right for you', I replied, 'but what about me? He was a professional pilot long before I went solo.'

'We've really got to hit the aiming point tonight', said Vin.

'Yes, and we can't afford to go for a Burton with the AOC on board', added Taffy darkly.

Our feelings were a mixture of relief and disappointment when, close to take-off time, the raid was cancelled.

On 16 April, two nights after we had gone to Stuttgart, we went on a long trip of over eight hours to attack the Skoda works at Pilzen in Czechoslovakia. We carried one 4,000lber and six Target Indicators, but first dropped flares over the target from 13,000ft. It was a long way to go over enemy territory, but the only trouble we had was when we were hit by flak over Karlsruhe on the return journey, the Jerries by then being thoroughly awake and hostile.

At about this time there was a tremendous flap on the station. We were told that distinguished visitors would be coming to see us the next day and that everything should be in spotless order. Later that afternoon, I was summoned to the office of our Squadron Commander, John Searby, or 'Honest John' as he was generally known.

'This mustn't go any further', he said, 'but our distinguished visitors are in fact Their Majesties King George VI and Queen Elizabeth. Your crew has been selected to be presented to them, but you are not allowed to tell your crew about this until tomorrow. You will parade in front of your aircraft for inspection by Their Majesties, and for Heaven's sake see that everything is polished up.'

I told a surprised crew that they were strictly forbidden to leave camp that night and should parade next day with clean uniforms and polished boots. A puzzled Tash had plenty to say about such unexpected requirements, but I gave him no room for argument.

Above left: RAW in his RAF uniform. (Wellington family archives)

Above right: RAW as a student at Harrow School. (Wellington family archives)

Scene from the farm in Atibaia, near São Paulo, Brazil. (Wellington family archives)

RAW driving a tractor on the farm. (Wellington family archives)

RAW with a prize bull. (Wellington family archives)

RAW during his early RAF training days with friends at a wedding. (Wellington family archives)

Right: Copy of pre-flight check list. (Wellington family archives)

Below left: Wing Commander Guy Gibson VC. (Wellington family archives)

Below right: Guy Gibson with colleagues. From left to right: P/O Frank Ruskell (navigator), P/O Johnny Wickins (rear gunner), Wing Cdr Guy Gibson (pilot), Sgt Gordon McGregor (second pilot), Sub Lt Gerard Muttrie (bomb aimer) and Flt Lt Brian Oliver (mid-upper gunner). (MOD Photograph CH 8469)

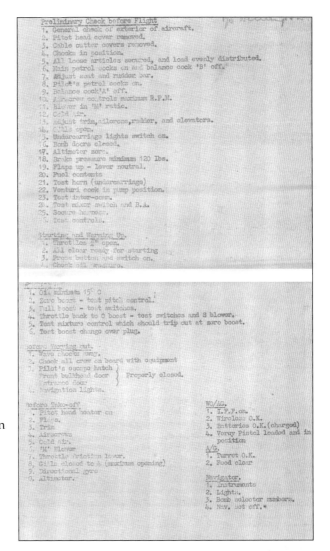

Preliminary Check before Flight
1. General check of exterior of aircraft.
2. Pitot head cover removed.
3. Cable cutter covers removed.
4. Chocks in position.
5. All loose articles secured, and load evenly distributed.
6. Main petrol cocks on and balance cock 'B' off.
7. Adjust seat and rudder bar.
8. Pilot's petrol cocks on.
9. Balance cock 'A' off.
10. Aircrew controls maximum R.P.M.
11. Blower in 'M' ratio.
12. Cold air.
13. Adjust trim, ailerons, rudder, and elevators.
14. Gills open.
15. Undercarriage lights switch on.
16. Bomb doors closed.
17. Altimeter zero.
18. Brake pressure minimum 120 lbs.
19. Flaps up – lever neutral.
20. Fuel contents.
21. Test horn (undercarriage)
22. Venturi cock in pump position.
23. Test inter-comm.
24. Test mixer switch and B.A.
25. Secure harness.
26. Test controls.

Starting and Warming Up.
1. Throttles 1" open.
2. All clear ready for starting
3. Press button and switch on.
4. Check all pressures.

[. . .]
1. Oil minimum 15° C
2. Zero boost – test pitch control.
3. Full boost – test switches.
4. Throttle back to 0 boost – test switches and S blower.
5. Test mixture control which should trip out at zero boost.
6. Test boost change over plug.

Before Taxiing out.
1. Wave chocks away.
2. Check all crew on board with equipment
3. Pilot's escape hatch } Properly closed.
   Front bulkhead door
   Entrance door
4. Navigation lights.

Before Take-off
1. Pitot head heater on
2. Flaps.
3. Trim
4. Airscrews
5. Cold air.
6. 'M' Blower
7. Throttle friction lever.
8. Gills closed to 4 (maximum opening)
9. Directional gyro
10. Altimeter.

W0/AG.
1. I.F.F. on.
2. Wireless O.K.
3. Batteries O.K. (charged)
4. Verey Pistol loaded and in position

A/G.
1. Turret O.K.
2. Food clear.

Navigator.
1. Instruments
2. Lights.
3. Bomb selector members.
4. Nav. set off.

Bomber Command officers and crews with a Lancaster aircraft (RAW is seated second from the right, third row from the bottom). (Wellington family archives)

RAW with 106 Squadron at Coningsby, May 1942. Top row, left to right: Vin Harley, bomb aimer/front gunner; RAW, pilot; P/O B.W. 'Bim' Bone, navigator; Flt Eng John Humphries. Bottom row, left to right: Sgt 'Nobby' Naylor, rear gunner; G.R. 'Titch' Webster, wireless operator; Sgt E. 'Ned' Needham, mid-upper gunner. (Wellington family archives)

Back on operations. Concentrated heavy and light flak over Bremen, 13 September 1942. (Wellington family archives)

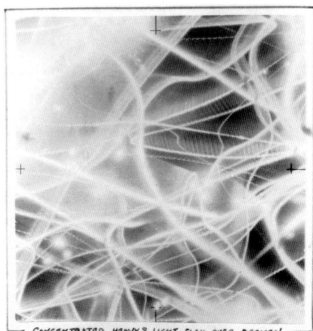

CONCENTRATED HEAVY & LIGHT FLAK OVER BREMEN
13. 9. 1942

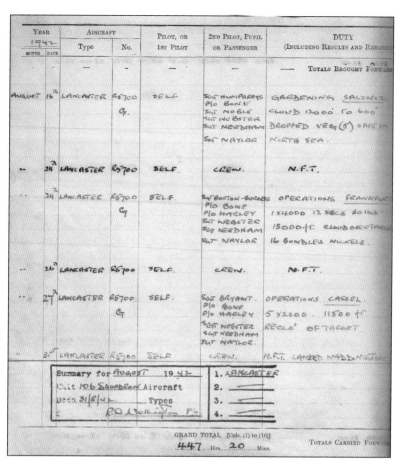

Two pages from RAW's log book, August 1942 (above) and January 1943 (below).

Mass daylight bombing raid by Lancasters on Le Creusot, 17 October 1942, in which RAW took part. (Wellington family archives)

Above left: Operation Genoa with list of crew, 22/23 October, 1942. (Wellington family archives).

Above right: A Lancaster in flight. (MOD Photo. CH.9131 (WF)).

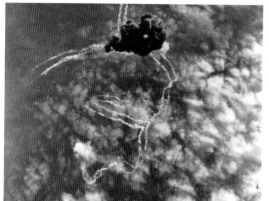
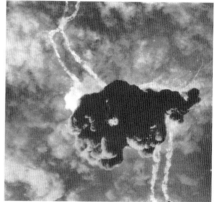

Above left: A Lancaster blows up after being hit by flak. The 'Grim Reaper' laughs out of the smoke. (Wellington family archives)

Above right: Detail of previous image.

Above left: Air Vice-Marshal Sir Arthur Harris with his PA, Walter Pretyman, and his daughter, Christina. (Pretyman family archives)

Above right: The Admiral Dumbo emblem painted on RAW's aircraft, showing twenty-seven completed bombing missions. (Wellington family archives)

A page from RAW's flight log book, January 1943. (Wellington family archives)

AIRCRAFT FLOWN

AIRCRAFT	ENGINE	AIRCRAFT	ENGINE	AIRCRAFT	ENGINE
MAGISTER.	GYPSY MAJOR				
OXFORD.	CHEETAH 10				
ANSON.	CHEETAH 9.				
TIGER MOTH	GIPSY MAJOR				
WELLINGTON	PEGASUS 18				
MANCHESTER.	VULTURE 2				
LANCASTER I	MERLIN XX				
PROCTOR. I					
MILES. MENTOR					
WHITNEY STRAIGHT					
MOTH MINOR.					
LANCASTER III	MERLIN 28				
HALIFAX	" 20.				
AVRO XIX	CHEETAH 15				
D.H.104 (DOVE)	GIPSY 71.				
RAPIDE (D.H.)	" 6.				
PROCTOR V					
STINSON VOYAGER					
STINSON RELIANT	LYCOMING.				
CHIPMUNK DC.1.	MAJOR 1 D				

Above left: Air Vice Marshal D.C.T. Bennett CBE, DSO, Chief of the Pathfinders, 1944. (Air Ministry Second World War Official Collection – CH 13645).

Above right: Pathfinder emblem – 'Strike to Defend'.

RAW and his crew with Sammy the spaniel in front of their Lancaster. (Wellington family archives)

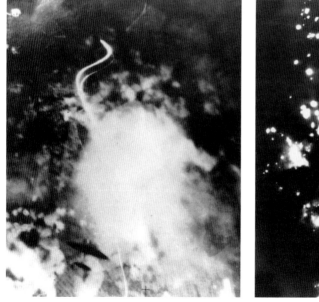

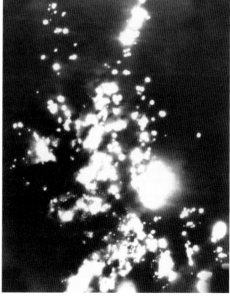

Above left: Photoflash over target. (Wellington family archives)

Above right: Pathfinder target indicators. (Wellington family archives)

Above left: Award of Pathfinder Force Badge, 26 June 1943. (Wellington family archives)

Above right: S/Ldr Wellington and crew represent 83 (B) Squadron at presentation of Pathfinders to King George VI and Queen Elizabeth, Wyton, 1943. (Wellington family archives)

YEAR		AIRCRAFT		PILOT, OR 1ST PILOT	2ND PILOT, PUPIL OR PASSENGER	DUTY (INCLUDING RESULTS AND REMARKS)		
MONTH	DATE	Type	No.					
		—	—	TARGETS. OPERATIONS.				
MAY	30	COLOGNE	4.20	OCT. 22	GENOA.	8.20	MAR. 12 ESSEN.	3.50
JUNE	1st	ESSEN.	4.10	" 24	MILAN	4.40	" 22 ST NAZAIRE	4.35
"	25	BREMEN	4.35	1942			AWAR 8 DUISBERG	4.50
"	29	BREMEN	4.20	JAN 3RD	ESSEN.	4.55	" 10 FRANKFURT	5.45
JULY	26	HAMBURG	5.35	" 8	DUISBERG	6.00	" 13 SPEZIA	9.00
"	30	DUSSELDORF	3.45	" 9	ESSEN.	5.00	" 14 STUTTGART	6.25
AUGUST	6	DUISBERG	3.10	" 11	ESSEN (RET)	3.20	" 16 PILSEN.	8.20
"	8	MINING.	5.30	"	ESSEN	5.55	" 26 DUISBERG.	4
"	11	MAINZ.	5.10	" 16	BERLIN.	8.40	MAY DORTMUND	6.05
"	12	MAINZ	5.15	" 16	BERLIN.	8.55	" 12 DUISBERG	4.30
"	15	DUSSELDORF	4.10	" 30	HAMBURG	6.30	" 25 DORTMUND	4.45
"	16	MINING	6.30	FEB. 13	LORENT.	4.30	" 27 WUPPERTAL	4.55
"	24	FRANKFURT	5.05	" 14	SPEZIA	8.45	JUNE 12 DUSSELDORF.	4.45
"	27	CASSEL	4.55	" 16	LORIENT	4.25	2ND TOUR COMPLETED	
SEPT	1st	SAARBRUCKEN	5.00	" 19	WILHELMSHAVEN	4.45		
"	10	DUSSELDORF.	2.30	" 24	BREMEN	4.40		
"	13	BREMEN	4.05	" 26	COLOGNE	4.45		
"	14	WILHELMSHAVEN	4.00	" 28	ST NAZAIRE	4.45		
"	16	ESSEN.	4.15	MAR 1	BERLIN	6.35		
"	19	MUNICH.	8.00	" 4	HAMBURG	5.10		
"	23	WISMAR	7.20	" 5	ESSEN.	3.50		
OCT	1st	WISMAR	7.05	" 8	NUREMBERG	7.15		
"	2	AACHEN.	5.40	" 9	MUNICH	7.10		
"	6	OSNABRUCK	5.20	" 11	STUTTGART	5.45		
"	17	LE CREUSOT	9.35					
				GRAND TOTAL [Cols. (1) to (10)]		TOTALS CARRIED FORWARD		
				........Hrs........Mins.				

A page from RAW's log book showing the different types of aircraft flown. (Wellington family archives)

A selection of press cuttings referring to RAW's official RAF lecture tour of Brazil. (Wellington family archives)

Above left: Civil marriage ceremony between RAW and Irene Smallbones, performed by her father, British Consul General Robert T. Smallbones, in São Paulo, Brazil on 15 February 1944. (Wellington family archives)

Above right: Wedding of RAW and Irene Smallbones, St Paul's Church, São Paulo, Brazil on 15 February 1944. (Wellington family archives)

Above left: Foreign military attachés, including RAW, presenting their credentials at the Palace of Belém, Lisbon, Portugal. (Wellington family archives)

Above right: RAW as Air Attaché in Lisbon, with his wife Irene. (Wellington family archives).

Igreja de N.ª S.ª da Ajuda, em Munique.

Hamburgo, Julho de 1943. Vitimas do terror aéreo britânico.

A guerra aérea anglo-americana contra a população civil alemã atingiu o seu ponto culminante com o método de „tapêtes de bombas"

„A defesa antiaérea tornara-se tão forte, que os bombardeamentos eram ineficazes, significando até um desperdício de energias. Os êxitos militares já não se equiparavam às perdas em homens e material. Para restaurar o equílibrio tivemos de utilizar bombas de tal efeito explosivo que, lançadas de grande altura, destruíssem o objectivo e um grande espaço em redor" (pág. 97).

„Em condições normais seria um suicídio para uma formação de bombardeiros, se quisesse sobrevoar o objectivo a uma altura donde pudesse fazer pontaria segura" (pág. 116).

Hitler não desejava que prosseguisse o bombardeamento mútuo

„...Não sabemos o que Hitler queria ou não queria, mas o que não queria, certamente, era que prosseguisse o bombardeamento mútuo. Opôs-se sempre a que êle começasse, e depois de ter começado, procurou aboli-lo" (pág. 47).

„Tapête de bombas"

German anti-RAF Bomber Command propaganda released in Portugal. (Wellington family archives)

RAW laying a wreath at the Portuguese War Memorial, Armistice Day, 1944 (Wellington family archives)

Above: Cartoon of RAW against an RAF flag, Lisbon, 1945. (Wellington family archives)

Left: Poster from Portuguese bullfight in honour of the victory of the United Nations, August 1945. (Wellington family archives)

RAF football team
arrives in Lisbon,
16 February 1946.
(Wellington family
archives).

Right: RAF and
Portuguese Army
football teams.
(Wellington family
archives)

Below: The players on
the pitch. (Wellington
family archives)

Oferta da
Companhia de Seguros "Comércio e Indústria"

Grupo do Exército Português				«Team» da R.A.F.		
	Azevedo				Williams	
	Sporting		Seleccionador		Wolverhampton	
Cardoso		Feliciano	Major Ribeiro dos Reis	Scott		Barker
Sporting		Belenenses		Arsenal		Huddersfield
Mateus	F. Ferreira	Serafim		Soo	Franklin	Paterson
Estoril	Benfica	Belenenses		Leicester	Stoke	Glasgow Celtic
	Quaresma	Salvador	Árbitro		Dougall	Brown
	Belenenses	Olhanense			Birmingham	Charlton
M. Coelho	Peyroteo	Rogério	De Lasalle	Matthews	Fenton	Smith
Belenenses	Sporting	Benfica	Francês	Stoke	Middlesbrough	Aston Villa
	Suplentes				Suplentes	
Valongo - Barrosa - Cabrita - Albano - Moreira				Hobbis — Shephard		
	Gôlos marcados por				Gôlos marcados por	

RESULTADO FINAL

Grupo Português: 1   Grupo da R. A. F.: 1

Above left: Queen Elizabeth the Queen Mother at the Pathfinder Association in London on 7 December 1961 looking at the photograph taken at Wyton in 1943. She is accompanied by (left to right) Air Vice-Marshal D.C.T. Bennett, who commanded the Pathfinder Force, RAW and one of his crew members, L.G. Johnson. (Wellington family archives)

Above right: Order of the Rio Branco awarded to RAW by the Brazilian government, 10 January 1969. (Wellington family archives)

RAF HARROWBEER
16 October 2009
The presentation of a commemorative plaque by the Brazilian Air Attaché, Col Cesar Estevam Barbosa and Cel Av Jordão. In recognition of the support by The Fellowship of the Bellows of Brazil to No 193 Squadron, RAF in providing nine Hawker Typhoon IB aircraft that were formally presented at RAF Harrowbeer on 16 October 1943, by the Brazilian Ambassador, Dr JJ Moniz de Aragão.

Presentation of a commemorative plaque by the Brazilian Air Attaché in recognition of the support received from the Fellowship of the Bellows of Brazil during the Second World War. (Wellington family archives)

'You get a proper shine on your buttons', I said, 'and tell Dusty to do the same.'

They were the only two NCOs in the crew now, since Connor, my mid-upper gunner, had left us about four trips previously. His place in the crew had been taken by Flight Lieutenant Johnny Johnson, an imperturbable, pipe-smoking type with plenty of wit and operational experience. At this stage Tommy, Vin and Johnny were Flight Lieutenants, Earl Reid was a Flying Officer and I was a Squadron Leader. Within three weeks both Tommy and Johnny received their promotions to Squadron Leader and Tash Goodwin his to Flight Sergeant.

We lined up in reasonable order on the tarmac in front of our Lancaster T for Tommy, serial number ED601, and soon the King and Queen, who had lunched with all the officers in the Mess, came across to us, accompanied by Don Bennett and John Searby. I had the honour of presenting my crew, who really looked quite smart. Even Tommy's cap looked less disreputable than usual, and Tash's language was impeccable for a change. We were an assorted bunch, consisting of one Australian, one American, one Canadian and four Englishmen, one of whom one (myself) had come from Brazil. An official photographer took a picture as I shook the Queen's hand, and almost twenty years afterwards this photograph was shown to her when, as Queen Mother, she came one evening to visit the Pathfinder Club in London. Rather on the lines of the programme 'This is Your Life', I was then taken up and presented to the Queen Mother as 'the officer in this photograph taken on that day in 1943 when Your Majesties visited RAF Wyton'. I think the Queen Mother rather enjoyed it: I certainly did, although, when she started asking me questions, I found myself almost tongue-tied.

My fifty-fifth trip was to Duisburg, and I thus had only five more operations to do. By the law of averages, a crew's last few trips, like their first few, seemed to hold a special element of danger, and many got the chop when a well-earned rest from operations was just around the corner. This dicing with death held a strange fascination, however, and the more experienced you became the better equipped you were to deal with conditions over enemy territory. No longer a sprog, you knew about flak and had learned to turn towards searchlight beams and dive through them instead of following your natural impulses to shy away. You knew full well the danger from enemy fighters and had your gunners constantly searching the sky above, below and on both sides of your Lancaster. Before take-off, the fear was always with you, like an aching tooth, but it subsided after take-off, just as the pain from an aching tooth usually subsides when you set off for the dentist's chair. Once you were airborne and en route to the target, then the only philosophy to adopt was, 'I'll do everything I can to avoid trouble, but if the enemy shell has got my name on it, then there's nothing to be done.' You could weave, search the sky and take every kind of evasive action, but none of this was any use against the lucky shot or a collision on a dark night. We once missed a Stirling by a hair's breadth. It suddenly loomed out of the dark a few feet in front of us and I just avoided a collision by hauling the stick back as Vin shouted a warning. Another second and we should have all had it.

Operational flying was nerve-testing, but relatively few aircrews went LMF. Anyone who had the misfortune to suffer from Lack of Moral Fibre was sent off to do what was euphemistically described as a 'refresher course' at Brighton. It was necessary for these unfortunates to be weeded out, because they could affect the morale of a whole operational crew. I had experienced this with a rear gunner who, as soon as we got over the target, began to say, 'Christ Almighty! Look at that flak! Jesus, that was close!' Such comments were, to say the least of it, worrying to the rest of us.

One evening, I had a harrowing experience with a sergeant from our squadron whose crew had been briefed to fly on operations that night. At the end of briefing, he came up to me, his face yellow and slimy with fear.

'Please don't let me fly tonight, sir', he said. 'I've got a wife and family and don't feel like flying tonight.'

I felt the only course of action was to be tough about it.

'What's the problem?'

'I don't think I'm up to it. Please take me off flying tonight. I haven't got the courage to tell my captain.'

'You go and fly tonight', I replied. 'I know how you feel, but if you can get through this op you'll find you are OK. You'll be sunk if you give up now. Once you take off it'll be all right, and you can relax over your bacon and egg in the morning when you get back.'

He gave me a strange look and walked away without saying another word. He and his crew were lost on operations that night.

There was a steady loss of crews, but they were always replaced. Of the old faces left on the squadron, I remember Val Moore, a tough New Zealander who was said to be always trying to do a slow roll in his Lanc, and Dennis Woolley, a very nice navigator I had known since we served on 106 Squadron together. There was a very good type called Squadron Leader C. A. J. Smith, or 'Smithy', who was also nearing the end of his second tour of operations. Each RAF Mess always seemed to produce a pianist, and Smithy was ours. He really could play beautifully and kept us all happy by playing our favourite tunes time and time again. He was always good-natured about it, even when, for the umpteenth time, I used to say, 'Come on, Smithy, what about having "As Time Goes By" just once more?' There was an amusing incident one evening in the briefing room, when the WAAF who chalked up the names of operational crews on the board wrote Smithy down as Squadron Leader D. Plunger-Smythe, for some reason which no one discovered. 'Well, if it isn't D. Plunger himself' was the sort of remark Smithy had to endure for some time afterwards. There was another pianist in the Mess who used to remove the sides of the piano before bashing out a really terrific rendering of 'Truckin'. It is amazing how our pianos stood up to it all; perhaps the pints of beer poured into them occasionally helped to keep them well lubricated.

Bombing methods had been changing, new equipment was being used, and as a result, our accuracy had improved considerably. The scientific gubbins were not always infallible, however. Before a raid on Hamburg, my crew and I were briefed to carry a special 'box' in our aircraft which, so we were told, would indicate the exact point at which we should release the markers and bombs.

'Your navigator will work this "box" and you must follow its instructions implicitly, whatever landmarks you may see on the ground', said the briefing officer.

We carried out our orders and came back to report that big fires had been started in the target area. Everyone thought it had been a good prang until the reconnaissance aircraft returned next day with the news that we had plastered a town some miles away from Hamburg and set the oil refineries there on fire.

We carried Gee, special equipment which enabled us to establish our position with considerable accuracy. The Germans jammed it, however, and as a result, its range was greatly reduced. Nevertheless, Gee was very useful for pinpointing your position over the English coast on return from a raid, or over the Channel before you reached it. Other aircraft on the squadron were carrying H2S, a radar aid which was proving very useful for navigation and bombing techniques. Its box and screen produced an outline of the ground and landmarks below, and the equipment was difficult to jam. The human element came in, however, because a trained operator was needed to work and read H2S. Since my crew had nearly finished operations, it was decided that there was no point in training us on this equipment.

Much of our really accurate marking on shorter trips, such as those to Happy Valley, was done by Pathfinder Mosquitoes carrying Oboe, which was equipment working to ground radar stations transmitting beams. Oboe was pretty hush-hush at that time, and I for one never learned anything about its technique of operation, even though the Mosquito crews using it were based with us at Wyton. What we did know was that they could mark a target through cloud to within an accuracy of about fifty yards error, something really startling.

Methods of attack varied, but generally the form was for the first Pathfinder aircraft to go in and mark the target with Target Indicator Reds or Greens, special bombs which exploded into cascading coloured balls on the ground, where they burned for several minutes. Before they went out, they had to be replenished by further Pathfinder aircraft for as long as the raid lasted. Aircraft of the Main Force came along at their allotted bombing times and aimed their loads at the burning TIs, thus achieving a good concentration. However, there was nearly always a creep back during the attack due to some Main Force crews dropping their bombs a little bit too early, or through faulty aiming. Pathfinder aircraft were detailed to re-mark the target if this occurred. On some occasions we also dropped a string of sky flares to mark a lane in to the target, but the disadvantage of this was that it helped enemy fighters to get at the bomber stream. With the flak, searchlights, flares and markers, the whole scene was often like a Brocks benefit.

We kept a particularly sharp lookout when friendly aircraft began getting close to us over enemy territory, not only because of the risk of collision but also because we had heard that the Germans were putting captured RAF aircraft into our bomber stream to shoot down unsuspecting crews. They were said to have made several crash-landed bombers serviceable and manned them with their own crews for this purpose. They could then creep up beside an RAF bomber returning home and give it a full broadside. This was definitely not cricket. One moonlit night, we had a terrific dogfight with a Stirling near the French coast on our way home. He aroused my suspicions by coming in too close, so I took evasive action and warned my gunners to be ready to shoot. The Stirling kept coming in and we got into tighter and tighter turns. In the light of day it would have been extraordinary to see these two great lumbering, four-engined bombers chasing each other round the sky in a heavyweight dogfight. I eventually got on the Stirling's tail and Vin gave him a squirt from the front turret, but he did not allow enough for deflection and our tracer went harmlessly just behind the Stirling's rear turret. This was enough to make him break off the engagement. We never did discover whether he was friend or foe. At our subsequent interrogation I reported this brush, but apparently, no Stirling crew complained of being shot at by a Lancaster on that particular night.

Recent orders to fly at 20,000ft or more, much higher than we were accustomed to, caused us engine and icing troubles as well as occasional failure of the oxygen supply system. I feel sure that Tash's oxygen must have packed up on the homeward journey from one raid. He suddenly announced that we had only enough petrol for another thirty minutes flying, which would not get us back to the English coast. I imagined that our tanks must have been holed over the target and started preliminary action for ditching in the sea; this meant breaking radio silence by calling up England to inform them of our difficulty and holding down the key of the set in order that they could get a fix on our position. Soon afterwards, RAF Air/Sea Rescue launches would set off for our estimated point of ditching in order to pick us out of the drink. The crew took up ditching stations in the aircraft and, as taught in training, were ready to clasp their hands together behind their necks at the moment of impact, since this was said to be the best way of taking the severe jolt which would occur when the aircraft hit the sea. They had already checked that our carrier pigeons, which we carried on all operational flights, were ready to hand in their cage for loading into the dinghy, if and when we ever got into it after ditching. The pigeons were important since they would carry home messages from us giving our estimated position once we were floating about on the sea. Normally the poor little devils got no attention from us, but now, in an emergency, they became valuable cargo.

By calling up base we had started an emergency operation involving a lot of people. In the operations room WAAFs would be trying to plot our position, the duty officer would have been on to the Air/Sea Rescue organizations, and even now launches were probably setting out to look for us. We were within about ten minutes of ditching time when I took a careful look at the petrol gauges. The main tanks were practically dry but the wing tanks were chockablock full; Tash, woozy from lack of oxygen, had forgotten to switch over to them. We cancelled the SOS message and got back with plenty of fuel to base, where I made abject apologies all round for the false alarm. The Air/Sea Rescue services were first class, and I felt very badly about getting them out on a wild goose chase.

On 4 May we were briefed to go to Dortmund and to bomb from 15,500ft with Target Indicator Reds, four 1,000lb bombs, one 4,000lb cookie and a 500lber. This was the substantial kind of load we could carry in Lancasters on shortish trips. Many people seemed to think that Pathfinder aircraft did not carry any bombs, but in fact we always carried a normal load as well as our markers. Telling evidence of this was given one night, when aircraft from the Pathfinder Group alone dropped a greater weight of bombs on Germany than the Jerries ever dropped in a single raid on Coventry. The tide had definitely turned by this time, and Goering's fatuous boast that no bombs would ever be dropped on Germany had certainly been exploded into smithereens. The Jerries were getting it back twofold, but they endured this ordeal with remarkable resilience, and one could not but feel a kind of admiration for the way in which they took it. I had been impressed one night to see the crew of an enemy anti-aircraft battery firing their gun even when there was a sea of flames all around them as a result of our bombing.

We had a good trip to Dortmund, but the trouble started when we got back to base and found it enveloped by filthy, swirling fog. We could see the airfield and flare path perfectly from 4,000ft, but when we got any lower the visibility became nil because of the beastly fog. Control told us to circle the beacon at 4,000ft, and we did so obediently for what seemed like hours. Many other aircraft were stacked up over the aerodrome and over the beacon, because no one could get down in these conditions. After a time some managed to land, and we were transferred from the beacon to circling the airfield. After another forty-five minutes, control tried to divert me to Scotland, but I replied that we had insufficient fuel to get there. The whole thing became a shambles. Aircraft started calling up saying that they had only a few minutes fuel left and that, if no permission to land was forthcoming, they would climb up after so many minutes to 6,000ft and bail out. The minutes went by, and then there were great flashes as the aircraft hit the ground. I was getting desperate, with only about ten minutes fuel left, and started to climb in order that we could bail out from a safe height.

Suddenly control called me up: 'Hello, T for Tommy, pancake.'

This permission to land was most welcome, but just as I was about to acknowledge it thankfully, a T for Tommy aircraft from another squadron replied to control saying that he was landing. This was worrying, but I was unable to sort it out with control with any success. There was nothing for it but to do a beam landing and hope that we avoided the other T for Tommy in the process. I got on the beam and ended up on the final approach with the right noises in my earphones, but with the visibility outside down to nil.

I called up the crew: 'I've got to listen to this bloody beam so stop any nattering and keep a good lookout.'

Clearly nervous about a blind landing, they relapsed into an uneasy silence. We heard the outer marker beacon noise at 700ft, but could still see nothing through the murk. We let down through the fog, and at 200ft the inner marker beacon sounded its insistent 'beep-beep' in our earphones. We had our undercarriage down and were coming in a bit too fast.

'The runway's dead ahead!' shouted Vin.

I saw it at that moment and pulled the throttles right back, ramming on full flap at the same time. It was not a good landing, but we got down in one piece. On pulling up at the end of the runway, I could see nothing because of the fog and had to call up control for a QDM or course to steer for dispersal. We parked the aircraft thankfully and then went off to interrogation, followed by supper in the Mess. We were eating our bacon and egg when the crew from the other T for Tommy aircraft came in to join us. They had crashed two fields back from the aerodrome in their Wellington, but all of them got out with nothing but minor scratches. If we had landed together there could have been an awful mess. Altogether, it had been a ghastly night. The Station radio control had been under tremendous pressure, and one of the WAAF RT operators had a nervous breakdown. Bad weather at base that night accounted for many of our losses, and I, for one, prayed that we should never have to go through the ordeal of another beam landing at night. As we had predicted, our new Squadron Commander, Wing Commander Gillman, failed to return from this op.

It was soon after this shocking trip that my father arrived in England on a visit from Brazil, where he was running a British railway. I got down to London for a brief moment to see him at the Great Eastern Hotel in Liverpool Street and arranged for him to make an unofficial visit to our station, something which civilians were not allowed to do under existing regulations. We broke even more regulations by smuggling him into our aircraft for a local flight, which promised to be something out of the ordinary. We had been briefed to send two squadron Lancasters to 'beat up' the town of Biggleswade, which was having a Wings for Victory Week, or Wings for Whisky Week as we irreverently called it. We were given permission to fly at low level over the town square during a period of five minutes, and it was hoped by officialdom that this display would encourage the inhabitants of Biggleswade to contribute generously to the fund being raised in their town. With my father safely aboard our aircraft, we set off with another Lancaster from the squadron formating on us. In due course we swooped low over Biggleswade and saw many people collected in the square. The weather was gusty, and this prevented us from doing any really low flying. However, I like to think we raised the dust in the main town square and shook the church steeple a bit. The other Lancaster peeled off after five minutes in accordance with instructions, but I was enjoying myself and stayed on for three quarters of an hour. It was great fun to be doing a 'beat-up' like this, and especially so with official blessing. A fighter, not wishing to miss the fun, formated on us a few inches off our starboard wing tip and stuck there throughout the performance. Eventually, we decided with reluctance that it was time to go home to our station. My father appeared to enjoy the Biggleswade experience, which was certainly an unusual one.

It was about this time that 617 Squadron, led by Wing Commander Guy Gibson, carried out the very successful and dramatic attack on the dams in Germany. We felt a great sense of pride in their achievement, and I for one felt sorry not to have been on the raid along with many old friends from 106 Squadron.

After going to Duisburg on 12 May, we had taken part in a heavy attack against Dortmund on 23 May, in which 2,000 tons of bombs were dropped. After this, we went to Wuppertal on 29 May, and I was then in the position of having only one trip to do in order to complete sixty operations and the end of a second tour. This was a frightening moment, because the last trip was often fatal to Bomber Command crews. It was surrounded with a kind of mystique, and one could sense that other squadron crews followed the outcome of other people's last trip with interest. The general question, thought but not spoken, was whether the crew concerned were going to get the chop or not. This provoked a sense of uneasiness, although one did everything possible to preserve an outwardly casual attitude to the final operation in order to disguise the turmoil of fear within. Most aircrews adopted an outwardly flippant attitude towards the dangers of operational flying as a kind of defence mechanism to prevent themselves from brooding on what was in fact a matter of life and death. We vied with each other in 'shooting lines', statements which usually made fun of the dangers by exaggerating them. The best-known classic of a 'line-shoot' was possibly, 'There I was, upside down with nothing on the clock but blood and the maker's name.' We kept a 'line book' in the Mess, and any good ones shot were immediately entered in it, the perpetrator of the 'line' usually having to buy a round of drinks for his disbelieving audience.

Our last trip was preceded by a period of prolonged agony of suspense, which tried our nerves to the last twang. On 4 June we were detailed for an operation that night and did our night-flying test in the afternoon in preparation for it. We were sitting in our Lancaster, getting ready for operational take-off, when control called up and said the raid was scrubbed because of bad weather. We returned grumbling to the Mess. The next night, and the night after that, we went through exactly the same routine. We were getting a bit het-up by this time, and Doc MacGown afterwards told me that at this stage my ears began to twitch. On 7 June we did a night-flying test and got prepared for the operation, but it was cancelled at the last moment. I began to despair of ever completing my operations. Two nights later, the same thing happened: we were ready to go but the operation was cancelled. The whole business had become a nightmare and altogether too bad to be true. On 11 June we finally got off the ground, taking Doc MacGown with us as an extra body, and went to Düsseldorf. This was about my eighteenth trip to Happy Valley, but though the reception was as hot as ever, we managed to weave successfully through the flak and searchlights and get a pretty good bombing run. I looked down at the fire and smoke in the target area with the thought that this was probably the last time I should ever be in this situation. My feelings were a curious mixture of relief at finishing and regret about not going on with this exciting business any more. My exercise in self-analysis was rudely interrupted by the receipt of a farewell present from Jerry in the form of a piece of flak that came through the windscreen just in front of me. Clearly, it was time to go home. We landed back at base without further trouble and, as we were taxiing to dispersal, the voice of Hobby, our RT controller, came through my earphones with a laconic 'Congratulations, Wimpy'. His words gave me a warm feeling of satisfaction, which could not be properly expressed in my brief reply of 'Thanks, Hobby, over and out'.

We got to the Mess at about four o'clock in the morning, and the party started immediately after our bacon and egg supper. For weeks we had been building up a large stock of bottled beer for this occasion and we set about demolishing it with thirsty determination, helped by those who had been on operations that night. Soon other officers got out of bed to join the party, and our pianist got cracking with the music. We had all the old favourites, and then Tommy and I sang an unusual version in duet of 'Miss Red Riding Hood'. The din went on as long as the beer lasted; Heaven knows what time it was when we went to bed, but it was broad daylight and the birds were singing.

After a week's leave, I was posted on 20 June 1943 to No. 8 (PFF) Group Headquarters in Huntingdon, where my new job as an operations officer would entail taking part in the planning and preparation of the Pathfinder Group's bombing operations. The prospect of a chair-polishing job was not exciting, but there was some consolation in the thought that I would remain in touch with operational squadrons and crews. It was rather sad, however, to think that our own little unit of a bomber crew had now disintegrated with the completion of operations so far as I was concerned. Tash safely finished his tour with other crews, and Tommy, I believe, went on to do a third one. Johnny Johnson subsequently came to Huntingdon as Group Gunnery Leader, but Vin Harley, Earl Reid and Dusty Hicks were afterwards posted elsewhere and I lost contact with them.

I made the last operational entries in my flying logbook and then totted up the totals, which gave 334.15 hours on night and 14.15 hours on daylight operations, all completed in just over a year. I was nearly twenty-four years old, an acting Squadron Leader and holder of the Distinguished Flying Cross, which had been awarded in March 1943 for service on 106 Squadron. Lady Luck had certainly been kind to me.

Chapter 8

Post-Operational Work

A summons came for me to attend an investiture at Buckingham Palace on 29 June 1943, and I had the honour of receiving my DFC from His Majesty King George VI. A host of us were collecting gongs on that day, and we were all equally nervous in case we did the wrong thing when walking up to the King. However, 'Speedy' Swift and other Palace experts explained the procedure carefully, and none of us muffed it. It was a wonderful ceremony to attend during the drabness of war days, and my recollections of the scene are of a mass of uniforms, what seemed to be acres of red carpet and a military orchestra playing my favourite music from 'Merrie England'. It was especially pleasing for me that my father, who was still in England, was able to go with me to the investiture and thus enjoy what for both of us was an unforgettable experience. The King was very charming and, after pinning the decoration on me, asked several questions about bombing operations.

After this delightful interlude, it was a case of getting back to the grindstone at PFF Headquarters in Huntingdon, where the work was very hard indeed. An officer by the name of Otto Altmann and I were the two Squadron Leader operations officers, and we each did shifts of twenty-fours on and twenty-four hours off. The shift of duty started at 0900 hours in the ops room, a large place with operational boards on the walls and a cluster of telephones on a huge table covered by a map of Europe under a Perspex sheet. The PFF Headquarters were installed in what had presumably once been a large private house, and the ops room, reached by a flight of steps leading down into it, had the size and height to have been a kind of baronial dining hall in more prosperous days. Other members of the operations staff sat up in a sort of small observation compartment and looked down at the scene of activity below, where WAAFs, male clerks and officers moved about on the task of planning, plotting positions and chalking up information on the blackboards. Things were usually quiet at the beginning of the day, until Bomber Command Headquarters, or the 'Petrified Forest' as we called it, came through on the telephone to say that operations were on that night, the target was so-and-so and the number of aircraft taking part in the attack would be so many. Now frenzy set in. Our first task was to let our own PFF Squadrons know which of them were required and how many aircraft from each had to be put on. There was then a Group conference, at which the method, route and timing of the Pathfinder effort was decided upon. Very often we had to plan simultaneous diversionary raids by our own Mosquito squadrons to make the enemy think that the main attack was going to some place other than the real target. We might also be sending some Mosquitoes independently on a 'milk-run' trip to Berlin, in order to allow the Jerries no respite. Pampa operations by our Met or weather-flight Mosquitoes over enemy territory had to be planned as well.

This planning business became more and more complicated as the war went on and new methods and techniques were introduced. Every operation was different, and details of bomb load, marking, armament, fuel, route, timing and so on had to be worked out for each one. It was vital to keep an eye on weather reports, since conditions over the target could make or mar a raid; fog or low cloud at base, moreover, might make it necessary to divert returning aircraft to other airfields, and the essence in such cases was for the ops officer to act quickly and book space at diversionary aerodromes where the weather was clear; if he left it too late, he would be liable to find that they were already fully booked by other Groups, and he was then in a fix when returning crews from his own Group demanded to be diverted somewhere. We were fortunate in having an AOC like Don Bennett to keep a close watch on operational planning and execution, since he could always be relied upon for sound advice and action, was prepared to stick his neck out and was not to be 'flannelled' with inaccurate information. I soon learned this one morning when he called me to his office and asked what the weather chart looked like. Not yet having looked at it, I tried to 'flannel' him by making vague statements about a cold front which would in all probability be lying on the route to the target, a guess I felt to be quite safe since there nearly always was a cold front in the way.

Whipping round on me, he said, 'Wimpy, you clearly have not yet looked at the weather chart. Go and look at it and then come back and tell me what the picture really is.'

I never tried it again and thereafter always admitted to ignorance if I did not know the answer to his questions. Talking of weather conditions, I cannot but pay tribute to our forecasters who, deprived of peacetime amenities, had to predict conditions long distances away over Europe, something they usually did with remarkable success. Theirs was a thankless task, since aircrews complained bitterly if forecasts were wrong but generally gave no credit to the weather pundits if they were right.

With the framework of the Pathfinder effort decided upon, it was left to the operations officer to sort out the details. We had to draw up a long document called a B Form, which was in fact the entire plan of our Group operation, with routes, bomb and target marker loads, zero hour minus and plus timing for aircraft, details of diversionary raids and so on. The B Form grew to be several feet long, and obviously, from a security point of view, it was vital that the information contained in it did not reach unauthorized persons. We had nightmares about losing it, and on one occasion there was panic in the operations room when the completed B Form was thought, wrongly as it turned out, to have been blown out of the window on a breezy summer's day into the streets of Huntingdon below. This all got magnified into an amusing story that our SASO (Senior Air Staff Officer) had been into the local fishmongers later the same day and discovered subsequently that his purchase was wrapped up in the B Form.

We had to consult right, left and centre to get the B Form agreed upon by all concerned, and then in the afternoon passed its details by scrambler telephone to all groups in Bomber Command and to the Petrified Forest itself. It made one feel rather important to read out the long epistle, product of a frantic morning's work, but once it was ended, the questioning by other groups began, which often led to telephonic arguments about operational details or suggested modifications. We had to keep our wits about us, but since we had, as it were, given birth to the B Form, we knew it sufficiently well to be able to cope with most questions about it. Nevertheless, the cut and thrust was often quite harrowing.

From now on it was plainer sailing, and the ops officer merely had to stand by the telephone to answer any queries and note any messages up to take-off time. From this vantage point one knew full well what intense activity was going on at bomber stations all over the country, with NFTs being flown, aircraft being bombed up, crews briefed and the hundred and one other preparations being made for the night's raid. These preparations could make it clear to people outside RAF stations that ops were on that night, but the important thing was to maintain secrecy about the name of the objective. Security was reasonably good on the whole, although the cynics claimed jokingly that one only had to ring up the pub called the Saracen's Head, or Snake Pit as it was then referred to by aircrews, in Lincoln to find out what the target was.

Pathfinder aircraft took off first in order to reach the target before the main force of bombers and mark the aiming points for them. Stations started telephoning the ops officer giving the times at which their aircraft had taken off, and all this information was chalked up on the operations board in group headquarters; during this time, the AOC or SASO would usually come in to see how things were going. After the aircraft had left there was a long pause, which gave the ops officer time for a sandwich and quick nap on the camp bed next to the telephone; any sleep he could snatch was welcome. There were WAAFs and other operations staff on duty who would wake him with a mug of tea at the required time, or beforehand in the event of any emergency.

When aircraft started to return a few hours later, the ops room became a hive of activity once again, and soon the telephone was ringing incessantly with squadrons passing their reports on the raid. Sometimes we attended the interrogation of aircrews at a station in order to ask them particular questions or merely to get a first-hand impression of the results of the raid. Back in the ops room, we noted down all the information and then prepared a first assessment of the operation, which we passed by telephone to Bomber Command. After this, we had to check with squadrons about stragglers coming back and then tot up how many of our aircraft were missing or at least overdue; it was sad to see the names of particular friends among them. By early morning it was all over, and you were glad to see your relief turning up at 0900 hours.

I recall two incidents during my time as an ops officer at PFF Group which illustrate Don Bennett's readiness to take an independent line for what he considered to be the best, although the course of action was contrary to orders laid down by higher authority. One night, the weather was absolutely lousy and it was clear that any bombers which returned from the target would have an awful job finding anywhere to land in England, Scotland or Wales, since the whole of the British Isles was cloaked with hideous murk. All the odds were on the operation being cancelled and, this being a foregone conclusion, Don Bennett instructed me to forbid any of our aircraft from taking off, even though the raid was still on and crews were at readiness. He was quite right, because aircraft which took off and then had to be recalled would have to jettison their loads of useful bombs in the North Sea before being able to land back at base with heavily-laden fuel tanks. However, Butch Harris was obviously determined that Bomber Command should attack Germany that night because, contrary to our expectations, the raid was not cancelled before take-off time. Aircraft from other groups took off, while all of ours remained on the ground. It became increasingly embarrassing for me to explain this fact to extremely senior officers when they telephoned to ask whether the Pathfinder Force would be on time at the target. My nails were nearly bitten down to the elbow by the time word eventually came through that the raid was cancelled and all aircraft must therefore be recalled to base. Don Bennett needed a lot of courage to do what he did, but his action meant that our aircraft had wasted neither petrol nor bombs and, also very importantly, our aircrews had been spared unproductive flying and the feeling of frustration caused by recall from an operation already embarked upon.

The other occasion was when a US Air Force General, I think it might have been Ira Eaker himself, spoke to me personally on the telephone and asked that one of our Met aircraft should fly over a particularly dangerous part of enemy territory at 1100 hours on the following day and bring back a weather report. On checking, it seemed to me that the whole thing was nonsense, because we understood that the American raid planned for the next day had already been cancelled in view of the rotten weather forecast. On Don Bennett's instructions, I telephoned the General and told him this, asking politely why he wanted us to risk an aircraft on this sortie. His reply astonished and annoyed me.

'Yes', he said, 'it's true that we have cancelled our operation. But I want an aircraft sent there to see what the weather would have been like had we carried out the operation.'

Don Bennett was as angry as I was about this, and I accordingly rang up the General and told him to go to blazes in the politest way that a mere Squadron Leader could convey such a message to a very high-ranking officer. Our relations with the US Air Force, who were based all around us, were generally very good, and this was the only occasion in my experience when there was some friction.

One day in July 1943, Don Bennett poked his head inside my office and said, 'Congratulations, Wimpy, on your immediate award of the DSO.'

I could only goggle at him and say, 'Good God, what on earth for?'

I certainly could not think that the award was for any personal deeds of derring-do and liked to think it was for combined crew effort over a period of operations. I was very touched by the arrival of a postagram dated 16 July 1943 from the Commander-in-Chief, Bomber Command and addressed to me personally with the text: 'My warmest congratulations on the award of your Distinguished Service Order. Signed A. T. Harris, Air Chief Marshal.' This struck me as an incredibly nice gesture on the part of the C-in-C and one that shows the degree of personal interest he took in the destinies of aircrew under his command. Implacable he may have been, and rightly so, about bombing Germany, but under that gruff and ruthless exterior there was undoubtedly a feeling of warmth and sympathy for the members of aircrew he sent out to do the job.

The strain of the twenty-four-hour work shifts was beginning to tell on me, especially as the off periods were often taken up not in catching up on sleep, but in catching a train to London and spending the evening at the Coconut Grove or some other nightclub. This routine entailed leaving the nightclub at four o'clock in the morning, when it closed, and catching the six o'clock milk train back to Huntingdon, which got me there in time to go on duty in the ops room at 0900 hours for the twenty-four-hour shift. It was a tiring and unhealthy life, and only the vigour of youth enabled me to keep up the pace for week after week. The operations work was stimulating and interesting, but some of the bureaucratic paper-pushing was intensely boring. At about this time, I was becoming exasperated by something called the operational record form, the completion of which kept me at my desk for hours at a time. The form demanded to know every single detail of each operational aircraft in the group during the previous month: at what time did it take off and to where, and what did it carry, were some of the questions contained in this hideous document of purely historical value. With the expenditure of much blood, sweat and tears I tussled with the form and, when the grim ordeal of completing it was finished, sent it off to a WAAF officer in Air Ministry who clearly received it with less than delight. Invariably, every month, she sent the form back to me enclosed with a cold letter saying that there were all kinds of mistakes, which would have to be corrected before the form could be resubmitted. And here we were with a war on. I finally lost my temper and decided to flummox the lady by getting the form completely right one month at the first time of submission. My sergeant and I spent hours acquiring a huge crop of information in order to fill up the form correctly for submission without blemish to the lady in London and keep her quiet. The day dawned when the form, checked, cross-checked, re-checked and checked again, lay on my desk for final perusal before signature and dispatch. I thought of the sleepless nights and uncomfortable days I had devoted to its completion and revelled in the thought that this time there could be nothing wrong with it. My sergeant and I sent it off and then repaired for a celebratory drink together, congratulating ourselves on a job well done. A few days later, the form came back to us with a letter from the WAAF officer; in substance this is what she wrote:

All the figures in this operational record form would appear to be correct. However, I note that you have secured the sheets together with steel paper clips whereas you must be fully aware that the regulations demand, for security reasons, that the sheets be secured together with brass paper clips. Will you please therefore rectify this error before resubmitting the form . . .

I gave up and wrote her a letter saying, 'To hell with those forms and the paper clips. Will you come and have dinner with me in London?' I got no reply.

The ops work did not mean that I was completely chair-bound, since on some off-days I was able to take small aircraft on short local flights and once managed to get in two and a half hours on a Halifax, a nice aeroplane but not, in my opinion, as good as the Lancaster where handling qualities were concerned.

On going through some assorted intelligence reports one morning in the office, I noticed a small bit of information stating that Goering would be spending the following weekend at a particular hunting lodge in Germany, and this seemed to me to present an ideal opportunity for dropping a 4,000lb cookie on him. I rushed off to Don Bennett and asked him for the loan of a Mosquito, arguing that a single aircraft of this type should stand a good chance of getting unmolested to the hunting lodge and back again by flying at low level all the way; having thought of the idea, I naturally claimed the right to do the trip. Later that day, the proposal was summarily turned down on the grounds that it was not our policy to mount planned attacks against individual enemy leaders. Disappointedly, I returned to the bumph on my desk and the pen-pushing routine.

In October or November 1943, the telephone on my desk tinkled and I picked it up, thinking that this would be just another of the hundred and one calls which came in throughout the day. But this one was strangely different.

After identifying himself, the caller said, 'How would you like to go on a lecture tour of Brazil?'

'Love to', I replied, without thinking of the implications.

Within a matter of days, I had left PFF Headquarters and found myself attached to the Ministry of Information in London, where Oliver Bonham Carter, who was then in charge of what was called something like the Latin American division, explained the plan of campaign to me. Two RAF officers would travel to South America and there give a series of lectures on the RAF, Squadron Leader Sandy MacDougall covering the Spanish-speaking countries, while I covered Brazil. We would leave together at the beginning of December by the *Queen Elizabeth*, then a troopship, and spend about a week with the British Overseas Press Service in New York before setting off by air for South America. In the meantime, we would get clued-up in London with material about the RAF which would serve as the basis for our lectures.

The whole thing sounded absolutely marvellous, but at this stage I thought it wise to point out that I for one had no experience whatever of giving lectures.

'Don't worry about that', was the airy reply. 'Flight Lieutenant Duxbury will give you some useful tips.'

It was not long before arrangements were made for me to meet Flight Lieutenant Duxbury at the cafeteria in Air Ministry. He turned out to be a nice man who had run a school of elocution before the war, but when I asked him what his present job was, he replied rather surprisingly that it was in a bomb-disposal squad. For a wild moment I wondered whether the principles of bomb-disposal were to be part of my training for giving lectures in South American, but it turned out that this was not the case. Over innumerable coffees, we talked about practically everything except the job in hand, and it was almost as an afterthought that Duxbury gave me a piece of paper listing the do's and don'ts for the would-be lecturer. The one which registered firmly in my mind was, 'Breathe when permissible'.

I was not getting very far with the preparation of subject matter for my lectures and pleaded with the Ministry of Information to tell me merely what I had to say, where I had to say it, when and to whom. Everyone was very charming, but I simply could not get satisfactory answers to these basic questions. There was nothing for it but to gather official data here and there and hope that the security-wallahs would not pounce on me later for saying something out of turn. My completed lecture notes, full of official facts and figures, seemed incredibly dull, and I could not visualize Brazilian audiences clinging spellbound to their seats while I spouted this sort of stuff. I buoyed myself up with the thought that it would be possible to consult our Embassy and consulates in Brazil before beginning my lecturing career in that country.

Sandy MacDougall and I caught the *Queen Elizabeth* in Greenock and found ourselves put in a cabin with twelve bunks in it; simultaneously, we made the shattering discovery that the ship was dry, because passengers were in the charge of an American Commandant. Sandy almost exploded with rage on hearing this and forthwith set out on a drink-acquiring sortie, from which he returned with three bottles of liquor, illegal cargo we had to secrete under the mattresses of our uncomfortable-looking bunks in the cabin. We were given only two meals a day on board, bars of chocolate serving as dinner in the evening, but there was some compensation in the fact that bread served with breakfast was delicious and astonishingly white compared with the greyish stuff we were accustomed to in wartime England. Sandy quickly crossed swords with the management at the time of our first lifeboat drill, when somebody shouted at us imperiously to get out on deck with all the other servicemen in uniform. Sandy, who cared about this more than I did, argued vehemently that we should be allowed to sit out lifeboat drill with civilian passengers in the snug atmosphere of the lounge, by virtue of the fact that we had diplomatic visas in our passports even though we were wearing RAF uniforms. He won his point, and thereafter we enjoyed the central heating and comfortable chairs of the lounge when other unfortunates paraded on deck in icy conditions for lifeboat drill.

The word soon got around that Noel Coward was on board, and dramatic, but no doubt inaccurate, reports quickly circulated to the effect that he was living in a specially silk-lined cabin, where flunkeys brought him supplies of iced champagne at regular intervals. Coward appeared at the farewell party on board before we got to New York and delighted us all with his own incomparable songs sung in his own magnificent way. 'Don't Let's Be Beastly to the Germans' made the ship rock with applause. He could not have had a more appreciative audience, and we could hardly bear to let him go back to that special cabin, which by now we hoped he had, together with limitless supplies of champagne.

Our voyage took about nine days, since we had to make a long detour to the north; at one stage, the experts told us that we were near to Iceland. We eventually sailed into New York, which was really a great sight for someone like myself who had never seen it before, the Empire State Building and concentration of other skyscrapers being even more towering than I had imagined from photographs. Sandy and I found ourselves on the dockside, a little bewildered by it all and wondering where we should go and stay. Nobody in London had given us any advice about this.

'Tell you what, Sandy', I said. 'I once saw an advertisement in an American magazine for some hotel in New York called the Waldorf Astoria, which looked pretty good.'

'All right', he replied. 'Let's try that one, and if it's no good we can always go somewhere else.'

The Waldorf Astoria certainly looked pretty good to us, and I could see that Sandy approved of my choice; I, on the other hand, was already wondering, after seeing the foyer, whether we had bitten off more than we could chew. We booked a double room and quickly learned that it would cost us nine dollars a night each without breakfast.

Sandy then inflated his chest in characteristic manner and said, 'But we can't possibly afford that because we are each receiving only nine dollars subsistence from the RAF for a night's accommodation and three meals. That means that we can pay for the hotel room and have nothing left over for food.'

The Waldorf Astoria people, bless them, took pity on us and very kindly reduced the price of our room to four dollars fifty a night each, a tremendous concession which I feel sure was made only because we were in uniform.

When we woke up next morning in our splendid room, Sandy and I decided to treat ourselves to the luxury of breakfast in bed and accordingly rang room service for ham and eggs and coffee. Shortly afterwards, a beautiful waitress wheeled in a trolley with all sorts of good things on it, including a packet of Camel cigarettes for each of us and what looked, by English standards of that time, like four newspapers, although it turned out to be only one copy; the amount of paper and print in comparison to wartime English dailies amazed us. After gorging ourselves, we suddenly caught sight of the bill: four dollars fifty each. This taught us a sharp lesson, and thereafter we took our breakfasts in a cafeteria for fifty cents or so.

We checked in at the offices of the British Overseas Press Service, housed on some incredibly high floor in a building on Rockefeller Plaza, and there met Hugh Macintosh, Jack Rennie and others, who looked after us very well during our stay in New York. Fortunately, we had just missed a strike of elevator boys which, during the period of negotiations, had forced the BOPS people to walk up to their offices, a journey on foot lasting forty-five minutes. We were told that, for obvious reason, such strikes were usually settled pretty quickly.

There were opportunities for us to go rubber-necking in this great city of skyscrapers, and we did not fail to go up the Empire State Building and visit Times Square, Broadway and Fifth Avenue. There was really no sign of a war on, and poor old London seemed very drab by comparison, especially where the shops were concerned. It was also strange for us, who had become accustomed to the blackout, to see so many lights about. The December cold was intense, but the insides of buildings were heated to what we considered to be hothouse temperatures, and entry into this atmosphere from the bitter cold of the street often gave me nosebleeds. I was very embarrassed one day, when looking at goods in Macy's, to have to suddenly rush out with a handkerchief clutched to my nose.

One day I had an odd experience in the Derby Tavern, a restaurant on Lexington Avenue run by an Irish ex-jockey and renowned for its steaks. I sat down at the bar next to a gentleman who looked exactly like a gangster. He was wearing a black hat just like gangsters wear in the films and a black overcoat with velvet on the lapels. He stared silently and fixedly at the back of the bar, and I thought it prudent not to engage him in conversation since he was obviously engaged in thoughts of his own. He did not make any movement other than to raise his glass and drain its contents with almost monotonous regularity. Not wishing to intrude on his meditations, I set down my empty glass with care and was about to leave when he suddenly said out of the side of his mouth, 'Have another drink.'

'That's really frightfully kind of you' I replied, 'but honestly you know I don't think I will.'

'I said, have another drink', he insisted, coldly and dangerously, and I accepted.

This routine happened twice, but at no other time was there any conversation between us. Finally, without any word, the man got to his feet and proceeded to walk straight through the plate glass entrance door to the place. I had not realized that he was completely plastered but, with that good fortune which so often attends drunks, he suffered no injury from the broken glass.

Sandy and I had unwisely drawn our subsistence money in advance, and the rate at which we were whooping it up in New York quickly caused it to dwindle at breakneck speed. Something had to be done quickly to improve our finances. I cannot remember how it was engineered, but somehow I found myself scheduled to appear on a radio programme called 'We the People', which was similar to the English 'In Town Tonight'. It consisted more or less of interviews with people who were in New York that week and thought to have something interesting to say. Our Embassy in Washington gave me clearance to appear on this programme, and as a result I was interviewed in advance by a green-visored editor with metal garters round his shirtsleeves in the approved American fashion. He was a man of few words, and none that he used made any mention of payment for my services. When I finally mentioned money rather delicately, he picked up the telephone and spoke to somebody connected with finance.

'Say, shower down on this guy', was all he said, but it meant that I would get fifty dollars for my pains.

I had imagined, quite wrongly as it turned out, that 'going on the programme' would mean no more than a couple of minutes work with the interviewer on the night. This was far from the case, since all of us who were scheduled to appear had to attend lengthy rehearsals, at which the interviewer treated us quite mercilessly in pursuit of getting the thing right. One of our number was an old man who had been President Lincoln's messenger and must have been ninety in the shade. When it came to his turn, the interviewer always extracted the last ounce of pathos with his final question, which was, 'And when was the last time you saw Mr Lincoln?' At this point, the poor old boy invariably dissolved into tears, because the last time he had seen Mr Lincoln was at his deathbed. It was real tear-jerking stuff, dramatic too, but I felt sorry for the old man in his obvious grief and angry with the interviewer for provoking this reaction.

Came the night, and we were all interviewed in turn under hideously bright lights in a large auditorium before a sizeable audience; scripts had been placed in our hands and we therefore had only to read out our replies obediently in response to the questions. I had fought desperately, but to no avail, about the text of my script, which had been written by someone who was clearly determined to lay on the drama about bombing Germany.

At one ghastly moment there was reference to a particular raid carried out against Munich at the time when Hitler was celebrating his birthday in that city, and I had to make some dreadful statement about 'lighting the candles on Hitler's birthday cake'. Those fifty dollars were hard-earned, but they certainly came in useful.

They did not last long in New York, however, but Sandy and I were saved from bankruptcy by another windfall. I was summoned to have lunch in a restaurant with Mr Randolph Hearst and a journalist called Bob Considine and, over some memorable clam chowder, was asked to write a story about bombing Germany for the magazine *Cosmopolitan*. The idea was for Bob and myself to get together about it, although he, as the professional, would do the actual writing of the story.

'I shall be prepared to pay you seven hundred dollars for the story', said Mr Hearst, and mention of this huge sum of money made me choke on the chowder. In those days, seven hundred dollars was, for an impecunious RAF officer, wealth beyond the dreams of avarice.

For the next day or two, Bob Considine, a thoroughly nice person, hounded me all over New York to get material for the story. One evening, he popped up beside me at a nightclub in Greenwich Village and talked casually about RAF bombing raids; we were on easy terms, and during the conversation I shot some fearful lines, one of them being about how dreadful the smell of flak was. Bob, as a good newshound, was of course taking note of everything and building up a good story. Next day, there was a second summons to lunch with Mr Hearst.

'I've reconsidered the amount I can pay you for that story', he said, and my heart sank to my boots; obviously that king's ransom was going to be reduced.

'Yes, I've been thinking about it', went on Mr Hearst, 'and have decided to pay you one thousand dollars.'

I could only numbly nod silent acquiescence.

The text of the story brought me back to earth, for it was written in such a dramatic way that I shuddered at the prospect of having to explain it to my crew if they ever saw it, which I prayed they did not. I complained bitterly about parts of the text, rewrote several passages and wrung solemn assurances that it would be published exactly as rewritten. With my morale somewhat restored, I left New York for Rio de Janeiro by Pan American Airways DC3 without having received the agreed sum of dollars, since there were bureaucratic delays before payment could be made. The money reached me six weeks later in Brazil, but alas, the US tax authorities had taken an enormous slice out of it. The story was published by *Cosmopolitan* without my corrections and this caused me a lot of later leg-pulling by my crew, who had somehow managed to get a copy of the magazine.

New York had been the parting of the ways for Sandy and me, since he had left there before me on a flight to the Spanish-speaking countries of South America; the moment when our separate lecture tours were to begin was getting frighteningly close. The flight by DC3 to Rio was leisurely by comparison with modern jet travel, and we must have taken nearly a week over the journey, going via Miami, Cuba, Haiti, Puerto Rico, Antigua, Trinidad, Belém and then down through Brazil. The long flying hours became boring, but nonetheless, it was rather a pleasant way of travelling, because you got to know the other passengers and had an opportunity to see something of interesting places where overnight stops were made. In Miami we spent the night in a strange house that had belonged at one time to Al Capone, and in Puerto Rico we spent the evening at a bogus kind of casino in a warehouse. The girls in Port-au-Prince were about the prettiest I had ever seen, but we were denied any chance of getting to know them better since we made only a short refuelling stop there.

The Captain of our DC3 was a tall, fair-haired type called Abrahamson, with whom I had long talks about wartime flying, either during overnight stops or when he came back from the cockpit to chat with the passengers. Evidently, he did not think that flying over the Channel or the North Sea amounted to much, even under operational conditions, and his theme was that no pilot was worth his salt until he had 'flown over the ocean'. This was rather irritating, but no amount of line-shooting about RAF raids budged him from the ocean requirement, and there was nothing for it but to agree to differ.

It was very exciting to land in Brazil once again, and indeed the projection from wartime England to flying down to Rio de Janeiro by commercial airline was almost unreal. On arrival there at the Santos Dumont airport I was met by my family, and we got snapped by Press photographers, a taste of what was in store for me on the forthcoming lecture tour, although I did not realize at the time how arduous were to be the trials that lay before me in this respect. The Air Attaché in Rio, Air Commodore R. W. Chappell MC, a really charming person, had nobly elected to accompany me on the tour and, in conjunction with the various Consuls concerned, had worked out our programme, which looked pretty formidable. The tour would cover the whole length of Brazil, with lectures at Belém, Fortaleza, Natal, Recife, Bahia, Rio de Janeiro, Belo Horizonte, São Paulo, Santos, Curitiba, Porto Alegre, Pelotas and Rio Grande in the south. It would mean giving lectures not only in Portuguese to Brazilian audiences in those places, but also in English to British communities and to personnel at American air bases, which had been established on the coast of Brazil for anti-submarine work over the South Atlantic. The whole tour would take something like five weeks of constant travelling, quite a stint, but at this stage I could only think that it would be Christmas in a couple of days' time and that the Air Attaché had given me permission to spend the holiday in São Paulo, on condition that I was back in Rio de Janeiro after the New Year to start the lecture tour on 6 January 1944.

I flew up to São Paulo by the commercial airline, which was operating 3-engine Junkers aircraft, and it was rather amusing when the pilot, who had a German name, invited me up front to fly the aircraft in my best RAF blue. In those days the flight took about three hours, but now it has been reduced to about sixty minutes.

It was wonderful to be back in my old room at my father's country house near São Paulo, to be welcomed by the servants and to wander round the stables accompanied by the excited dogs, but disconcerting to find that my civilian clothes preserved in the cupboard from pre-war days were too tight for me now. I was exceptionally lucky to be enjoying such home delights, which were denied to most servicemen in the UK who had joined up from abroad.

There were many friends to look up during the short period of leave and, most important of all, there was a particular girl I wanted to see again. We had gone around together quite a lot in São Paulo before I joined up, and the long separation that followed had not altered my strong feeling that she was the girl for me. We now saw each other again at a cocktail party, but the meeting was not exactly charged with romance since she dug me in the ribs and said I had got fat, while I said I refused to take her out to dinner that evening unless she removed her ridiculous hat, which had strange antenna-like objects sprouting from it. She gave in eventually and went hatless with me to have dinner at a small French restaurant called La Popotte, followed by dancing at the Jequitibá nightclub. The blissful few days we spent getting engaged passed all too quickly, and all too soon I had to report to the Air Attaché for the start of the lecture tour.

Chapter 9

Lecture Tour

Roy Chappell and I left Rio de Janeiro at crack of dawn on 6 January 1944 by Brazilian commercial airline for the north of Brazil and arrived in the afternoon at Belém, capital of the State of Pará, which was where the lecture tour was to begin. Belém, situated near the Equator and at the mouth of the Amazon River, was muggily hot, and we sweated uncomfortably in our uniforms. The locals there claimed that it rained punctually every day at 3.00 pm and that appointments in the afternoon were arranged, not at stipulated times, but for either before or after the rain.

We were met on arrival by HM Consul Mr Gurney and an RAF officer stationed at the air base, who took us to the Grande Hotel in town where, shortly afterwards, officers from the FAB (Brazilian Air Force) paid an official call on us. In stifling heat, we attended a cocktail party given by the American Consul and then had dinner with him, a meal that was enlivened by his French wife, who decried us mere men by constantly repeating the phrase, 'Ze man, he is no good; ze woman, she make ze France.'

Our first official call at an early hour next morning was on the Commander of the Brazilian Air Force base, where we were received by a band before meeting the officers and being shown round the airfield and installations. After this, we called on the Admiral of the Amazon and then on the Mayor, drinking little cups of ceremonial black coffee all along the line. After visiting the American air base in the afternoon, we called at the small RAF Signals Unit, which was housed in a small shack at the edge of the airfield. We could not but compare their living and working conditions with those of the Americans, who had every comfort, including mosquito netting on all buildings and an abundance of refrigerators filled with Coca Cola. We returned to the hotel in a tropical rainstorm and got drenched.

The dreaded moment arrived that evening when I had to give my first lecture in Portuguese, the mere thought of which had been keeping me awake at nights. As zero hour approached, I regretted having accepted the invitation to go on a lecture tour and wished myself back on the mundane job of completing operational record forms at PFF headquarters. However, I was now at grips with reality, and reality had me in a stranglehold. At the appointed hour I found myself sitting at a table in an upper room of the hotel before an audience of Brazilian Air Force officers. My delivery of the lecture was simply appalling, because sheer nervousness made me gallop through a forty-five-minute talk in twenty minutes, thus committing the crime of verbal acceleration from which beginners are prone to suffer. Matters were not helped by the failure of the electric lights after a few minutes, which left me with a pile of paper and a bewildered expression in the guttering light of a candle. I tried to appease my audience with MOI propaganda photographs, but they had seen them several months previously and treated them with polite scorn. The whole affair was a terrible flop, and afterwards the Air Attaché, the Consul and I tried to relieve our depression by drinking large iced gin and tonics at the little tables outside the hotel. My companions were glumly silent, and I could sense that their unspoken thoughts were, 'My God, what have we let ourselves in for?'

At ten o'clock the following morning we received a call from the Admiral of the Amazon, who was accompanied by a bevy of satellites simply dripping with gold braid; after polite conversation and the inevitable cups of black coffee, they beat a dignified retreat. This left us free of any official engagement until the evening, when we went to a cocktail party at the Consul's house and met the British colony, numbering five souls. It was nice to talk English to them as we all mopped our brows in the Amazon heat.

I was booked to give a lecture at 9.00 pm that evening in the Palacio do Comercio, and the authorities had promised faithfully to turn on the electric current a few minutes before the time of starting, a promise they adhered to. By now, I had learned to reduce the verbal pace and, taking all in all, the lecture was quite a success. We felt quite pleased when, after hasty goodbyes, we caught the midnight plane for Fortaleza and watched the lights of Belém recede behind us.

Our arrival at Fortaleza took place at the ungodly hour of 5.15 am on 9 January, but the Consul, local authorities and Americans from the local air base were there to meet us. The Americans gave us a wonderful breakfast of ham and eggs but, before we were through with it, insisted on dragging us off to see their pride and joy, a Blimp used for anti-submarine patrols. The sight of the great bulbous thing at that early hour of the morning filled me with less than emotion and I depressed our host by remarking, 'God, what a beautiful target!' Relations between us were a little strained after that.

We drove into town and installed ourselves in quite a nice little hotel, which was fanned by a constant, cooling breeze, a characteristic of Fortaleza. By now, Roy Chappell and I wanted more than anything to sleep, and we each retired thankfully to bed for a rest before the next part of the official programme. After two minutes, there was a knock at my door and a reporter, accompanied by his photographers, burst in despite my remonstrations. They insisted that I get dressed but, after heated arguments, I compromised by putting on tunic and scarf over my pyjamas in order to pose for the shot.

After a pleasant luncheon with the British Consul, we met the British colony in the afternoon, an exercise that was well worthwhile. Sometimes no more than a handful of people in an outlying place, these colonies were all helping Britain's war effort in any way they could, whether by keeping British concerns going in difficult conditions, working for the Red Cross or contributing in other ways. By the end of the trip I was loaded down with woollen comforters of every kind, gloves, scarves and balaclavas, as well as woolly jobs to keep my knees warm. Many of these people had sons, daughters or sweethearts serving with the forces round the world and, though they never said it, I realized how much they must long to have their loved ones out on the sort of visit I was lucky enough to be making to Brazil. The worst moments were when mothers told me that their sons had gone missing on flying operations and asked me what chance I thought they had of being safe. One could only try to give comfort and, above all, hope, by quoting cases where others had returned safely or been made prisoners of war after long silences.

In the evening, we set off for the American air base, where I gave a lecture in English in an open-air theatre; it didn't go too badly, although I feel sure that we were all far more anxious to watch the Betty Grable film that followed.

The next day's programme began with a courtesy call on the American Consul, followed by a lecture in Portuguese at the local Army barracks; in the evening, we had drinks at the Country Club before moving on for an official dinner at a charming place on the beach called the Jangada Club. 'Jangada' is the name of the fishing craft used in north-east Brazil; they consist of nothing more than logs tied together, but move pretty fast under their triangular sails, most of the log platform being awash. Certainly, they must be seaworthy, for the fishermen have no hesitation in taking them miles out of sight of land.

Fanned by balmy tropical breezes, we dined in the open air on the club verandah and, as we listened to the sea breaking on the shore and the wind rustling the palm trees, it seemed to me that this lecture tour was not such a hardship after all. The food was excellent, the wine copious and the company pleasant, altogether a combination to make any man forget the problems of tomorrow. The prize dish of the evening was delicious and, turning to our Brazilian host, I complimented him on it and asked circumspectly what it was.

'Donkey', he replied, perfectly seriously.

The steady cascade of wine had made us all exceedingly eloquent and, at the end of the meal, we vied with each in delivering flowery speeches containing frequent expressions of mutual admiration. Pleased with ourselves, we settled back contentedly over the cigars, but were electrified when the barman suddenly and unexpectedly launched into an impassioned speech about bombs on Berlin, reaching heights of oratory far superior to anything that had gone before. Acknowledging that we had met, not our match, but our master, we clapped him to the echo as he modestly retired to take up his position behind the bar once again. We got to bed at midnight after this magnificent finale to the Fortaleza visit.

Rude awakening came at 4.00 am, when we had to catch the plane for Natal where, after arrival, we repaired to the Grande Hotel for breakfast. The British Consul came to call on us and told us the programme, where upon I wilted visibly, since it was formidable; this business of giving lectures, calling on officials and being constantly entertained was already proving to be quite exhausting in the intense heat. The Consul told us the hotel accommodation left much to be desired and took us off to stay instead in rooms which had been arranged for us at a hospital run by nuns, this being the place, he said, where visitors in transit usually stayed.

After meeting the British colony in the evening, we moved on to the bar of the Grande Hotel, where we met a charming Canadian called Doctor Wilson, a great authority on malaria and yellow fever. He was a most amusing character and proceeded to do some conjuring tricks which had us all amazed. To end the show, he called for a live cockerel and, within a matter of minutes, the barman hurried back with a fine, though somewhat truculent specimen. Doc Wilson soon hypnotized it by first putting its head under its wing and then stroking the neck feathers; in a short time it was out for the count, and we were able to roll the bird round the table without it showing any reaction. After we had all made this experiment, Doc Wilson took its head out from under the wing and, after shaking itself, the cockerel strutted off as truculently as it had come on stage. After this unforgettable performance we went on to the local casino, which unfortunately proved to be rather unpleasant and slightly bogus.

Next morning, 12 January, we made the usual calls on the local authorities before I gave a lecture at the Brazilian Air Force base, where the extremely friendly and hospitable officers took us to their Mess afterwards for refreshments. In the evening, there was a drinks party given by the British Consul, and then at 8.00 pm I did a fifteen-minute broadcast on the local radio.

On the following morning we visited the American air base, one of the most important ones on the Brazilian coast at that time, and after lunch there I gave another lecture. We returned to the hospital feeling that, if the present pace lasted, we should soon have to enter it as patients needing a long period of rest. At 8.00 pm we proceeded to the local theatre, where a band blared in the foyer until the arrival of the Governor. We were then herded with the bigwigs to a table on the stage and sat down beside a great barrage of flowers, with an immense audience in front of us. Suddenly, a quiet-looking little man sitting next to me sprang to his feet and delivered the most oracular speech I had ever heard. He accompanied the flight of oratory with eloquent gestures of the hands. Having spun round several times and nearly fallen off the stage, he returned to his seat amidst a thunder of applause. Completely eclipsed by this introduction, I delivered my lecture.

We left at 8.15 am next morning by plane for Recife, where we arrived about one hour later. As we stepped out of the plane, we were met by Brazilian

Air Force officers and a full-blown brass band playing in our honour. On return to the hotel from official calls made in the afternoon, we became involved in everlasting interviews with the press. Tedious though it was, we did our best to satisfy them, because they had given us marvellous coverage since the beginning of the tour, treatment they kept up right to the end.

More official calls followed next morning and then, after I had done a broadcast on the local radio, we escaped for our first afternoon off to bathe at Boa Viagem beach as guests of Wilfred Shorto and his charming wife. It was a wonderfully soothing break from the official routine and helped to condition us for the trials still to come. The following afternoon was actually rather fun, as we took tea at the English Club while watching a cricket match, which was all rather incongruous in that heat, but terribly British nevertheless. After the match, I gave a talk in English to the community and then went off to a dance at the American Club, where the guest of the evening was Ilona Massey. We had to admit that she was a far greater attraction than cricket.

The main engagement next day was at 8.30 pm. in the theatre, where I was due to give a lecture in Portuguese. Quite a mob of us, including the local priests and soldiery, sat on the platform, which was covered with a forest of white lilies, and the whole business was rather formal. The heat was stupendous, and we returned later to the hotel in an exhausted condition, only to find that reporters were waiting for us with their pads and pencils at the ready.

'In the RAF, do you have a professional lecturer who travels about the various stations talking to the aircrews about politics?' was one of the questions they asked.

'I've never heard of such a thing', I replied, much mystified.

'Then how do you know what you are fighting for?' they demanded triumphantly.

We had to get up at 4.30 am next morning to go to the airport, our plane for Bahia (now Salvador) being scheduled to leave at 7.00 am. The brass band was there to play us off and got into the groove with a really lively samba as we made our salutes and goodbyes.

The lecture tour had not gone too badly so far, but I did feel that the text of my talk, full of statistical figures, was extremely dull pudding for

Brazilian audiences who, I had gathered in conversation, were far more interested in the human side of a bomber pilot's life than in tonnage of bombs dropped between the years so and so. I sat up most of that night rewriting my lecture and was pleased with the result; all the statistics went overboard and the new version described a bombing raid from the moment a crew heard they were on operations until they returned to base, simple language being used throughout. The Ministry of Information might not have approved of the new text, but I felt perfectly certain that this was the sort of stuff my listeners wanted to hear.

One of our official calls made during the day had been on the Army General commanding the area, a gentleman who obviously did not approve of pilots. Ostentatiously fingering his staff officer's badge, he said to me, 'Intellectuals should not be wasted as pilots; they must be kept as staff officers.'

At the end of a tiring day I gave a lecture to the British community who, like all the other communities we had met, were touchingly interested to hear details of the war effort in England.

Next morning, I gave a lecture at the American air base and in the afternoon was interviewed at the hotel by six newspapermen. There was an official dinner that evening at the Consul's house, and one of the guests was the General who had laid so much emphasis on the need for intellectuals to be retained as staff officers.

When accepting the invitation to dinner, he had said, 'Thank you very much. I will tell my wife to get my false teeth in good order.'

Sitting next to him at table I felt that his wife must have lost his teeth altogether, since he toyed miserably with a plate of potato salad. When the meal was over, we left for the Associação de Comercio (Commercial Association), where the new version of my lecture, simultaneously broadcast live in the main square by means of loudspeakers, was quite a success.

Next morning, 20 January, we set out in a taxi run on alcohol, petrol being short in Brazil, for the air base at Ipitanga, a journey normally lasting about forty minutes. After fifteen minutes the taxi broke down irrevocably, and there was nothing for it but to thumb a lift from a passing lorry. After this inglorious arrival at our destination, I gave a lecture to

the Americans in their theatre and immediately afterwards crossed over to
the Brazilian Air Force base on the other side of the airfield, where I had
to give a talk in Portuguese. By this time my throat was getting extremely
sore from so much talking, and the Air Attaché accordingly decided to cut
out our visit to Vitoria, the next port of call down the coast. He telegraphed
this decision to the Press Attaché in Rio and in reply received a bleat about
carrying out our programme as planned, the desirability of sticking to it
and so on. Roy Chappell then retaliated with the following signal, which
effectively silenced the Embassy: 'We are going direct to Rio. Wellington is
not repeat not a performing bear.'

This exchange of signals caused quite a sensation in the Embassy,
so much so that a wit there was inspired to write the following verses:

> Warning: The Lion has wings
> They welcome Tiny everywhere
> And flock round him in millions;
> He's suffering from the wear and tear
> Of talking to Brazilians;
> But, dear admirers, do beware;
> Our Tiny's not a performing bear!
>
> He is our local lion now
> And fair Jemima's fancy;
> But he hasn't a moment anyhow
> To talk to his fiancée!
> He's sick of doing the smile and bow
> And the time has come to make a row!
>
> On Goering he kept dropping in
> Till sixty times he'd bombed Berlin;
> He'd sooner do it again for choice
> Then lecture till he's lost his voice!
> For tho' he's a lion, he's got quite hoarse
> And now can't boost the Royal Air Force.

(When his throat's sore a lion can't roar –
And whispering's such a God-awful bore!)

So the Air Attaché's had to declare
That Tiny's NOT a performing bear!

By cutting out the visit to Vitoria, we obtained four days rest for ourselves, and it was not until 25 January that we started the programme in Rio de Janeiro with a luncheon at the Halfway House (Anglo-American Club), followed by two or three more lectures during the next few days. The one I enjoyed giving most was to members of the Fellowship of the Bellows, an organization whose members subscribed a fixed sum of money every time a German aircraft was shot down, the proceeds going towards paying for Spitfires and other aircraft for the RAF. Members wore lapel badges in the form of a bellows, and the colour of the badge reflected the amount that the wearer had contributed, gold ones being worn by top-notch contributors. This splendid band of patriots collected a fantastic amount of money for Britain's war effort in the air; as evidence of this, I can remember an occasion when the Brazilian Ambassador in London handed over a Typhoon squadron to the RAF which had been provided out of funds raised by the Fellowship of the Bellows. These people really did a magnificent job of work but, in my opinion, their effort did not receive the publicity it deserved, perhaps for the reason that they did not want it.

HBM's Ambassador Sir Noel Charles attended this particular lecture, which was enthusiastically introduced by Dr Herbert Moses, the President of the Brazilian Press Association and always a staunch friend of Britain. Need I blush if I say that the auditorium was packed with an attentive gathering of Fellow Bellows? The whole affair was rather a success and I, for a change, enjoyed every minute of it. Afterwards, we went to the home of Sir Henry Lynch for a very pleasant dinner, which was attended by the Brazilian Air Minister and his ADCs. The whole evening was arranged with characteristic grace and charm by Sir Henry, who was one of the nicest people imaginable and a true friend.

The Air Attaché and I were ready at 4.00 am next morning to catch the plane for Belo Horizonte, but we struck it off our list of visits on learning that the airport there was under water, thus making the flight impossible for an indeterminate time. We left for São Paulo instead, and there I gave lectures to the Brazilian Air Force and the British community, as well as one to the British Legion at a Dugout Supper. One of the most enjoyable events was a large luncheon given by the Fellowship of the Bellows at the Esplanada Hotel, an occasion graced by the presence of the governor and other authorities and at which a piece of a Heinkel shot down by the RAF was on view. São Paulo was home ground for me, but my problem there, not met anywhere else, was how to get rid of a personal bodyguard detailed by the police authorities to watch over me night and day, a service that was hampering, to say the least, for someone like myself who had only recently become engaged. It was off-putting to have the guard treading on my heels everywhere, but finally, after a heart to heart talk, he agreed to push off and abandon me, with some reluctance, to my fate. We drove down to the port of Santos where, after an official dinner, I gave a lecture in the Atlantic cinema, which was packed with about two thousand people. My original terror of public speaking had, by dint of considerable practice, become less by now, but this particular evening was a real ordeal because the air-conditioning system broke down almost immediately, with the result that the heat inside the cinema was tremendous.

The next port of call was Curitiba, capital of the State of Parana, where a large German colony had been established for many years. The Vice Consul, Blass Gomm and his wife Luisa looked after us very well, and she, one of the first Brazilian women to qualify as a pilot, even took me up for an exciting half-hour in a two-seater aeroplane on a sightseeing tour. There was an amusing incident during a party given by the Belgian Consul and his wife, when three self-confessed Nazi guests, obviously bubbling with anger, glared at us as we wandered round the delightful garden picking grapes here and there.

Finally, unable to contain himself, one of them came up to me and said, 'Did you know that the Allies shot down sixty-three German transport aircraft in North Africa the other day within a few minutes?'

'Yes', I replied. 'That was a darned good show.'

'Good show for the Allies!' he spat at me with a thoroughly dirty look.

This exchange annoyed us all, and so the wife of the Belgian Consul thereupon made a pointed speech of welcome to the RAF at the end of which I kissed her roundly on both cheeks. This was too much for the Nazis, who immediately collected their hats and departed.

We had wondered what our reception would be like in Porto Alegre, the next stop on our itinerary, because the German influence there was really strong. Would they throw hand grenades or rotten eggs, or merely boycott the lectures? Surprisingly enough, it was the best reception I got on the entire tour; indeed, it was difficult to leave the theatre afterwards because of the pressing throng of well-wishers and autograph hunters.

From here we went to Pelotas, a small town in the centre of a large cattle-breeding area. We were met by Mr Lamb, manager of the Frigorífico Anglo (Vestey's) plant there, and by the local Mayor. The latter, a venerable old man with a keen sense of humour, took charge of us and helped with the various calls to be made.

After a Rotary Club luncheon, we went to call on the Aero Club, where our arrival caused chaos, since they were expecting us only the next day. After the preliminary confusion had been overcome, however, champagne corks flew and speeches were made.

The next call was on the Army. We arrived there earlier than expected and found them in the process of practising the national anthem and march past in our honour. Slight chaos resulted, but the ensuing time taken in re-arranging the troops was filled most satisfactorily with toasts in champagne.

We left them to call on the cavalry, who were ready for us. We inspected the guard of honour and were then taken to an upper room, where we again drank champagne. We were feeling fairly merry on the stuff by now. Suddenly, the Air Attaché sprang to his feet and delivered a rousing speech in English. Churchill could not have done better. As we all applauded loudly, the Air Attaché turned round and ordered me to translate his speech into Portuguese.

This was definitely not cricket, and my effort resulted in about half a dozen ineffectual words, which were a pale reflection of the heights of oratory just achieved by the Air Attaché.

Feeling on the crest of the wave, we pressed on to the Palacio do Comercio to meet the local bigwigs, who also gave us champagne. After being photographed several times we went on to a cocktail party with the British Colony. That evening, I gave a lecture in Portuguese at the local library.

The end was now in sight, since only a visit to the town of Rio Grande remained in our programme. We drove there by car and went through the usual routine of calls and lectures and parties. On 11 February we caught a train for Pelotas and were given a great send-off at the railway station. Even the Captain of the Port appeared and distributed highly-smelling cigars.

At Pelotas we caught a train for Porto Alegre, where I had to give a lecture, the very last one, at the Country Club. On 12 February we caught a plane to São Paulo, and that was the end of the lecture tour, thank goodness.

I think it was a success, but certainly the past few weeks had imposed a tremendous physical and mental strain. It was my great good fortune to go round the course with Roy Chappell, who had proved to be the kindest and most equable of companions as well as being a most understanding senior officer. Poor man, he must have become heartily sick of my same old lectures after listening to them time and time again, but he never showed any signs of boredom, irritability or impatience. His performance, often in the face of fearful odds, earned my unqualified respect, loyalty and friendship.

Chapter 10

Getting Married

The next thing was to get married. Before the lecture tour my fiancée, named Irene but known as Pussy, and I had agreed that 15 February should be our wedding day, and this was only three days away by the time I got back to São Paulo from the south. However, all the arrangements seemed to be beautifully under control and everything had been fixed for us to get married at the São Paulo Consulate General in the morning and then at St Paul's Church in the afternoon. Pussy's parents, Mr and Mrs Smallbones, would be giving a large reception afterwards at their home in the Rua Maranhão, and from there we would take off to spend our honeymoon at my farm near Atibaia, about fifty miles from São Paulo.

The only thing that worried me was that my defective ear had been playing up and had caused me several fits of dizziness during the lecture tour, especially when standing at the salute in the hot sun for minutes on end. I therefore went off to see my ear doctor, a marvellous man called Cicero Jones, who was descended from one of the Confederate families which settled at a place called Vila Americana near São Paulo after the American Civil War.

Cicero examined me and said he would have to perform a mastoidectomy as soon as my honeymoon was over. Only afterwards did he confess that he wanted to operate immediately because my ear was in a bad way, but decided to take a chance on leaving it a bit longer. When he did operate later he found that part of my brain was exposed.

Our wedding day arrived and the Consul General performed the civil ceremony. It was really rather a distinction to be married by one's father-in-law. Hundreds of friends came to our church marriage and to the reception afterwards. My wife and I finally left for the farm in a huge Cadillac car driven, since there was no petrol in those days, by *gazogenio*. This consisted of two charcoal ovens mounted on the back of the car which by some mysterious process made it go but with very reduced performance. One could not get far without topping up with charcoal and altogether it was a messy process. Anyway, we got there and had a lovely honeymoon.

No sooner was it over than Cicero Jones had me in the Samaritano Hospital, where he spent three and a half hours carving me up on the operating table. I remember vividly the feeling of terror I had on coming round from the anaesthetic, because I was convinced I had crashed in my Lancaster and was trapped inside it. The safety harness held me immovably in the pilot's seat as the aircraft caught fire and I yelled to Vin and Tommy for help. The safety harness was of course nothing more than the straps holding me to the hospital bed. It was a horribly painful operation. All the doctors at the hospital were old friends, and six of them helped Cicero with the operation in one way or another. Neither Cicero nor any of the others ever charged a penny for the operation but said they had given their services as a small contribution to the war effort. Subsequently, I managed to get the Air Ministry to write them a letter of thanks. They were really wonderful people at that hospital, and no one could have treated me with more tender care than Willy, the German male nurse.

Flying home to England was out of the question, and so it was decided that I should be invalided home by ship with my wife accompanying me. We received orders from the Embassy to catch the SS *Croix*, which turned out to be a somewhat elderly French passenger boat. One of the few good points about it was that we could get really good champagne at four shillings a bottle.

The Brazilian Navy escorted us part of the way up the coast from Rio de Janeiro and then left us to our own devices. I asked the Captain whether we should be joining a convoy, but he replied that we should be making 'a quick dash' on our own across the South Atlantic to the coast of Africa, where we would pick up an escort. I asked what the top speed of the ship was for this quick dash and he replied 'seven knots'.

It looked like being a dangerous passage as the German U-boats were very active on our route. Moreover, we soon discovered that the political sympathies of the ship's company were divided. The officers were for Free France, while the sailors were mainly Vichy sympathizers and had ideas of commandeering the ship and sailing it into a Vichy port. It was an uncomfortable situation on board. The passengers consisted of a few male and female British volunteers, families and a large number of young children. We also had a handful of British Merchant Navy captains, good types all, who were being repatriated after their ships had been torpedoed. We drew up a plan of action for an emergency but had little with which to take on the Vichy crew in the event of trouble, since our total armament consisted, if I remember rightly, of one service revolver.

Surprisingly, our quick dash across the South Atlantic was accomplished with success, and we never saw the smallest sign of a German U-boat, though we were all pretty uneasy during the voyage. We whiled away the time by having long talks with the ship's doctor and with one of the Merchant Navy captains called Cameron, who told us nostalgically about the beauties of heather whisky produced near his home on the Island of Islay. The food on board was good and unlimited.

One hot morning, we came on deck to see a low coastline ahead of us, and soon we anchored off Freetown. We should have liked to stretch our legs ashore, however unattractive the place looked, but this was not allowed. Our moment of excitement came when first a Royal Navy, then an Army and finally an RAF launch came out to our ship bringing members of these services who would be travelling with us back to England. We were delighted to see these welcome reinforcements, but the faces of the Vichy crew became longer as more and more British servicemen came on board. There could be no question of their taking over the ship now, and the change of situation made their surliness to us give way to politeness. They now got out of our way when we met on the decks.

Our ship was overcrowded with passengers, but we soon settled down together. We felt much safer in every way, especially as we now joined a convoy for the journey home. My wife continued to play backgammon with Carrie Davis, who had been my father-in-law's secretary at the Consulate General in São Paulo before embarking with us in Brazil, but there were new people to meet and talk to. In particular, I remember Flight Lieutenant John King from Stow-on-the-Wold, who became a good friend, and also a nice RAF padre.

We were well equipped with men of God, since there was also a Royal Navy padre and a missionary and his wife travelling with us. A bit of a problem was created for them some days later when one of the crew died. We all expected the missionary to take the burial service, but he refused to do so as the dead man had been a Quaker. We all took an extremely poor view of the missionary, but he remained adamant. The question now was who should take it. Technically speaking, the Royal Navy padre probably should have done so by virtue of his being the senior service, but he and the RAF padre got together and decided that the latter should do it as his French was a little better. He practised the words and was reasonably fluent by the time we put on our uniforms and paraded for the burial service. Everyone turned out except the missionary, who during the ceremony ostentatiously walked round the deck in sports clothes accompanied by his wife. I am sure some of us began to wish we were burying him.

The whole service was moving but rather extraordinary, because the RAF padre had hardly begun before another crew member, the ship's cook I think, sprang up to him, snatched the book from his hand and read the rest of the service. It came to an end, and the canvas-encased body was sent over the side on its lonely journey into the sea, a moment I found rather shattering from an emotional point of view, even though the dead man was unknown to me.

The rest of the voyage was uneventful, except when our aircraft-carrier escort lost an aircraft over the Bay of Biscay for reasons unknown. It could have been due to weather, engine failure or an unfortunate meeting with a Jerry. The most cheerful moment was when we heard on the BBC that the Allies had invaded Europe. The tide was obviously turning with a vengeance, and we all felt elated to hear this wonderful news.

Finally, we sailed into Greenock, and it was good after the long voyage to be at rest alongside, to hear the gulls screaming and all the other sounds of a busy port. It was nice to be back in wartime England, or rather Scotland. Somewhat befuddled after the farewell party of the night before, we prepared to meet the Customs at crack of dawn. We had brought quite a lot of trunks and boxes with us from Brazil, and what was worrying me was how to explain to the Customs that we had 168 pairs of silk stockings with us.

Just before we left São Paulo, a friend had said, 'I understand that silk stockings are very difficult to come by in England. I have a factory here making them and would like to give you a few pairs for distribution to whoever you think fit. This will be a very small contribution from me to the war effort.'

We replied that naturally we should be delighted to take them, and expected to be sent half a dozen pairs. My wife and I were simply flabbergasted when he sent round 168 pairs, which would probably make us the biggest single owners of silk stockings in the British Isles at that stage, when practically none were available.

The Customs officer started his questioning, and I confessed to a bottle of sherry here and some cigarettes there. He appeared not to be interested and in fact left our cabin while we were rummaging around for other goods to declare. Running after him, I said we had forgotten to show him a case in which there were 168 pairs of silk stockings, explaining how we had acquired them. Giving me a look of complete disbelief, he turned on his heel and walked away. He must have thought I was trying to pull his leg and clearly disliked such flippancy at an early hour of the morning.

We got ourselves to London and went to stay with an old and dear friend called Oscar Oppenheimer at his flat in Hertford Street. Uncle Oscar, as he was known to many, had been persuaded by my father-in-law, then Consul General in Frankfurt, to leave there before the war and settle in England to avoid being put in a concentration camp. One of the kindest elderly gentlemen imaginable, Uncle Oscar was looked after by his faithful housekeeper Anna, who was a superlative cook. I had first been taken to the Hertford Street flat about two years before by Peter Smallbones, my future brother-in-law, before he was killed while serving with the Army in Egypt. Since then, Uncle Oscar had often given me meals and a haven during periodic visits to London on leave. Even during the most difficult times of rationing Uncle Oscar never failed, in my experience, to have a bottle of whisky and fifty cigarettes on his table to offer his guests. I never discovered how he acquired them, but Anna told me he made occasional journeys by taxi to mysterious parts of London to call on his suppliers. During the Blitz, the authorities had tried to evacuate Uncle Oscar to the country, but within a matter of hours he and Anna were back at the flat in London and never moved again for the entire war. He was a most generous and wonderful person, who allowed us to trespass hugely on his hospitality.

Pussy and I arrived at Hertford Street during the nasty period of the V-1 flying bombs and found that Uncle Oscar had been persuaded to move out of his bedroom, where there was a lot of plate glass, and sleep on a camp bed in a passage. With cheerful warnings about the glass, he offered us his bedroom as temporary quarters, and we accepted. I must confess that on many occasions when the flying bombs were overhead that great area of glass seemed too close for comfort and we scurried out of the bedroom to stand in the passage. I hated the flying bombs and was scared stiff every time their motors stopped overhead, because you never knew if they were going to glide on or drop on your head. I think they and the V-2s were more wearing on the nerves that the straight bombing in the Blitz.

My first task was to report to Air Ministry doctors at Hallam Street to see how my ear was getting on. It was just my bad luck to fall into the hands of a very senior Ear, Nose and Throat specialist who had grounded me a long time previously and who was clearly very annoyed to find that, contrary to his ruling, I had persuaded others of his more junior colleagues to allow me to continue operational flying. And now I was in his office as a post-mastoidectomy patient who had been operated on in faraway Brazil, something that seemed also to raise his ire. My ear had healed up nicely, but he now jabbed at it painfully until it bled. I shall never forgive him that performance. At the end of the ordeal, he instructed me to report to him regularly, adding the warning that if I did not do so, he would send and have me brought there. The way he said it made the whole silly thing sound as though I would be dragged in irons to the torture chamber. I had to go back to that detestable man, who was the only RAF officer I ever disliked. It was quite obvious that he would do everything in his power to prevent me ever getting into the air again and, sure enough, at the end of the treatment I was pronounced unfit for flying.

By this time, my wife and I had moved into a not very nice little flat in Curzon Street, which was relatively cheap as it was up on the fourth floor and nearer the flying bombs. It was probably a combination of four flights of stairs, the flying bombs and sheer worry that caused her to start a miscarriage. I got her into hospital, but we lost the baby.

We were both acutely depressed by what had happened, but suddenly things started to brighten up for us. I was summoned to an interview with an Air Commodore and was very intrigued to know what it was all about. The interview was really rather funny, because the flying bombs got closer and closer as I stood in the Air Commodore's office, and both of us evidently shared a keen desire to get behind a convenient screen as protection against the glass being blown in. Being only a Squadron Leader, I had to wait for my senior officer to move first. Finally, when a V-1 came right over the building, the Air Commodore retreated rapidly behind the screen with me hot on his heels. After a time, we emerged and the interview began.

'We've decided to send you as Air Attaché in Panama', said the Air Commodore.

My face fell a mile, and he looked at me in surprise.

'But what's wrong with that? After all, you speak good Portuguese.'

'Yes, sir', I replied. 'But they don't speak Portuguese in Panama.'

'Good Lord. Where do they speak Portuguese?'

'Portugal, sir.'

'Very well', he replied. 'You will go as Air Attaché to Portugal.'

And so it was decided that I should go to Lisbon towards the end of August (1944) after a period of briefings and attachments in London. I rushed home to tell the exciting news to my wife, and we agreed that this was a splendid job to get now that I was unfit for flying.

I think the Air Commodore must have had a moment of mental aberration when he said Panama instead of Portugal, or perhaps muddled me with another officer who was indeed sent as Air Attaché to Panama. After all, he was the Director of Allied and Foreign Liaison and knew his geography and languages extremely well.

My round of attachments and briefings started under the able and sympathetic direction of Mr J. B. Hogan, who was the redoubtable civil servant in charge of the office responsible for the welfare and destinies of all Air Attachés. It was hard but interesting work. One problem was that security regulations prevented us from telling any of our family or friends that we were going to Lisbon. Another problem was how to get some civilian clothes made at a fortnight's notice. A friend from the Brazilian

Embassy gave me the name of a tailor in Clifford Street, who proved most cooperative although I had never been there before. I ordered a new uniform, tails and two or three suits, which they produced two days before the deadline. It was odd to be going to wear civvies again after four years in uniform. And just the thought of turning out again in white tie and tails was quite fantastic.

Chapter 11

Lisbon

It was difficult for us to imagine what life in neutral Lisbon was going to be like after wartime England. Its reputation at that time of being a key listening post in Europe for Allies and Germans alike was most intriguing, and from hearsay it sounded as though there were spies behind every potted aspidistra in Estoril. And for people accustomed to the blackout, it was also going to be quite extraordinary to live in a fully lit-up city.

I understood I should be taking over a staff consisting of two Assistant Air Attachés, both Flight Lieutenants, a secretary and a team of eight non-commissioned RAF wireless operators engaged on transmitting important weather reports. By this time I had been promoted to Acting Wing Commander, which was the rank then of the Air Attaché in Lisbon. I should be taking over from Jack Schreiber and accordingly wrote him the usual letter saying that the present Air Ministry living allowance for Lisbon was £3 a day and did he think this was enough to live on. It would be all that we should have apart from my pay. Jack wrote back saying that the allowance was perfectly adequate, and this sounded most encouraging. At the same time, he said, there was a fully-furnished flat in the Avenida Tenente Valadim in Lisbon available at £45 per month, and he asked whether we should like to take it because, if so, he could reserve it for us against our arrival. The details sounded extremely good and, being a greenhorn in those days, I signalled acceptance.

Our preparations became more and more frantic during the last few days before departure, but finally we were ready to comply with the Air Ministry travel instructions for going to Lisbon. At that time, flights carrying passengers between England and Lisbon were being operated by KLM crews under British control, and much security surrounded the time and place of departure of the DC3 aircraft used on the service. It had not been so long before that Leslie Howard had vanished on one of these flights returning from Lisbon. We left from Hurn and had to spend the previous night, if I remember rightly, at the Sandbanks Hotel in or near Bournemouth.

We took off on the evening of 30 August 1944 and made a tremendous detour well away from land in order to avoid Jerry aircraft. There was little comfort aboard the DC3, and we passengers were so much cattle. At least some rather good coffee was provided en route from huge Thermos flasks and this kept us going for the ten hours or so that the journey took. Soon after daybreak, we were flying over a typical Portuguese cork and olive tree-studded countryside and then we came in to land at the Portela airport in Lisbon. It was rather hot and everything seemed very strange. Jack Schreiber met us, deposited us in an enormous and palatial double room at the Aviz Hotel and left us to sleep off the effects of the journey.

After waking up, I investigated the Aviz Hotel and was most impressed. Great Danes belonging to the owners lay about in the reception rooms, and the whole establishment, with about only twenty-five bedrooms, looked more like a lavish private house than a hotel. I inquired the price of our room, and the resulting shock was such that we moved out the same day into humbler quarters. Nevertheless, we afterwards became greatly attached to the Aviz and had many meals there in surroundings that probably did not exist anywhere else in Europe at the time. I seem to recall that Senhor Rugoni, a very charming man, was one of the owners.

A diminutive Portuguese taxi – many of them were small Austins in those days – took me to our Chancery in the old part of Lisbon on a sloping street called the São Domingos à Lapa, where I called on Jack Schreiber to discuss the work and running of the office. When I asked him again whether the allowances were adequate, he shattered me by replying that they were perfectly adequate but you had to be prepared, of course, to spend about £1,000 a year of your own money.

'I believe the Military Attaché manages to live on his allowances', he added.

I was rendered speechless with stupefaction and rage. He appeared to be a rich man, but I certainly was not. He was the kind of man who would think less of you, I believe, if you confessed that you did not have £1,000 a year to supplement Air Ministry allowances.

He introduced me to the Assistant Air Attaché, Geoffrey Stow, a splendid fellow who became a lifelong friend, and to the other Assistant Air Attaché, William Aldridge, together with his weather wireless operator teams. My secretary, Miss Wyatt, who seemed a bit dour on first acquaintance, proved to be an absolute jewel, and I soon discovered that she was simply invaluable. To be honest, I think she was responsible for the efficient working of the entire office.

Our Ambassador was Sir Ronald Campbell, a diplomat of the old school who wore black coat and striped trousers and was at first somewhat forbidding. However, both he and his wife were absolute poppets and a joy to serve under. They always did the right thing at the right time, and the feeling of certainty that they would react perfectly in any situation gave a great sense of confidence and well-being to their staff. Any rockets they gave were well-deserved and received in good part.

Our Embassy was staffed by exceptionally nice people such as Ian Wilson-Young, the Head of Chancery, Admiral Bradley, the Naval Attaché, Ashley Clarke, the Minister, Brigadier Rex Barter, the Military Attaché, and a host of other good men and true. Also, we were exceptionally lucky to serve together with Marcus Cheke, then the Ambassador's personal assistant, who earned a high reputation for the books he wrote about Portugal. We were devoted to Marcus and his wife Connie, and Marcus taught me many things, including the wisest procedure to be adopted while on a shoot in Portugal.

'Get behind the biggest tree', he said, 'because the beaters are armed and come towards you firing their guns.'

We often went together on the craziest of picnics, and I particularly remember one when we set off in riding clothes to try out horses in the north of Portugal, but ended up picking mushrooms by moonlight somewhere not far from Lisbon without getting anywhere near our planned destination.

We moved into our flat in the Avenida Valadim and it was not long before we discovered that the place was infested with lice, which was no doubt the main reason for the lowish rent. They crawled everywhere, and none of the normal methods could dislodge them. Although the official decontamination squad adopted such dramatic measures as burning our mattresses, the lice survived, and we accordingly looked for accommodation elsewhere. Eventually, we took rather a nice little doll's house in the Travessa do Patrocinio in the Bairro da Estrella, which was charming in a Chelsea sort of way, although the main disadvantage was that one could not get into any bedroom without going through another.

Work in the office was quite hectic, and one of my major problems was the granting of priorities to passengers travelling by aircraft back to England by the KLM-operated DC3 services, which came under my jurisdiction. Miss Wyatt controlled the normal issue of priorities quite admirably, but when cases were awkward she referred them to me. As a result, it was not uncommon for me to find tearful ladies in my office pleading that their husbands, brothers or sweethearts should be allowed to fly home because of their duodenal ulcers or whatever. It was a bit harrowing to turn down some applications, and on more than one occasion I felt a complete cad about doing so. However, these priorities were few in number and had to be dished out sparingly to only really deserving cases. The trouble was that every case seemed to be more deserving than the last.

Life in Lisbon then was great fun and almost completely divorced from the realities of war. We had taken over Jack Schreiber's cook, said to be the best in Lisbon, and in addition employed a first-class parlourmaid, a housemaid and a washerwoman. The sum total of their combined monthly wages added up to the equivalent of £10. However, nearly everything else was expensive and, in particular, I remember that our monthly electricity bill was usually in the neighbourhood of £25, a large chunk out of my living allowance. The food was marvellous after rationed England, and the shops were full of things we had not seen for ages. We were darned lucky and made the most of it.

I had been supplied by the Air Ministry with a large, camouflaged, desert-model Humber motorcar, and so we often drove away to the countryside at weekends for picnics in the cork forests or to bathe in the icy sea at Arrabida, which was then a deserted spot. Another excursion was to Caldas da Rainha, 100 kilometres north of Lisbon, where there was a nice fair, and then on to the nearby sea resort called Foz de Arelho, where there was a comfortable hotel run by an Englishman. On some occasions we went with 'Bouncer' Reynolds, who was the Embassy lawyer, to spend the weekend at Estremoz in the Alentejo, where his brother Victor lived in a lovely old country house in the middle of a property where there was plenty of shooting. We shot hares and also red-leg partridge, or Frenchmen as they were known there, which were extremely difficult to hit as they came whistling over the cork trees. At lunchtime on these shoots we repaired to a peasant's whitewashed cottage and had a delicious meal washed down with gallons of red wine. No one could be a worse shot than I, but these lunches, and more probably the red wine, improved my performance no end, for in the afternoon I seemed hardly to miss anything and brought off lefts and rights that amazed myself. We had many pleasant evenings round Victor's generous table with charcoal braziers under it to keep us warm.

Once we spent the weekend at Evora, also in the Alentejo, and walking round that whitewashed town by moonlight was an experience I shall never forget. The narrow, crooked streets were just as one imagined they had been in the sixteenth century, and it was easy to visualize bygone scenes of swordplay in the twisting lanes and auto-da-fé processions in the main square. The hotel where we stayed had once been the palace of the Inquisition; there were still dungeons down below and, so people said, the sounds of groans coming from them. One thought of the wretches who had suffered torture and turned uneasily in bed at night wondering if their ghosts still walked the stone-flagged passages at midnight. Day dispelled the creepiness, and Evora was beautiful once more.

We got to know interesting people in Lisbon such as the Gulbenkians. Calouste ('Mr Five Per Cent') Gulbenkian lived at the Aviz Hotel and his wife in Estoril, but they used to meet once a week. He was a small man and allegedly had a specially high chair at the corner table in the Aviz Hotel restaurant, where he habitually took his meals. He apparently had a fear of being poisoned and could often be seen grating carrots at table. Madame Gulbenkian was a large, dominating and not very beautiful lady, who was an absolute sweetie once you got to know her. She was slightly deaf but seemed to hear everything when she wanted to. The first time we met was at a cocktail party and she beckoned me with an imperious finger saying, 'Come here, young man. I wish to speak to you.' I went, and we became firm friends thereafter. We also got to know her son Nubar in Lisbon, one of the nicest people you could ever meet, and he was a dear friend of ours until his death.

The Duke and Duchess of Palmela were a really charming couple. He was Portuguese Ambassador in London at the time and often flew out to Lisbon and back by our DC3 service. He was an inveterate smoker who felt the altitude during these flights, and so I arranged for him to have a supply of oxygen every time he flew. They had a very large family, and I remember going to dinner with them one evening at their house in Cascais. Palmela had said beforehand, 'It is only family', but we were shaken to see the dinner table laid for about fourteen. We thought it might be an official dinner party after all, but it turned out that there were only the Duke and Duchess, their many children, the family priest and ourselves.

The British and German embassy offices were very close to each other, and so were the residences of the two ambassadors. There was an amusing story about a new British Embassy secretary who was bidden by his Ambassador to dinner immediately after his arrival in Lisbon. He took a taxi to what he thought was the right destination and entered a house where a large reception was in progress. It seemed to be a good party, but everybody was speaking German. Everyone seemed to avoid him, until after a time a man took him off to a small room and said, 'I think perhaps you were looking for the British Embassy and have made a mistake. This is the German Embassy.' Apparently he then saw him off the premises quite charmingly. The British secretary in question told me he was acutely embarrassed to find that he had picked up dog's mess on his shoes outside the German Embassy on the pavement, and clearly it was the aroma that had made people give him a wide berth at the party, not necessarily his nationality.

The German Service Attachés had their offices just down the road from our Embassy, but we did not run into them very often. When doing so, we naturally cut each other dead. My opposite number there was Colonel Hashagen, a man considerably older than myself and rather a decent looking type. At one stage I felt sure the Colonel was following me about, since he kept popping up with a pair of field-glasses, even when I was playing a round of golf at Estoril. I cannot think what he hoped to achieve by keeping such a close eye on me. Incidentally, we Service Attachés wore civvies nearly all of the time and only put on uniforms for official calls or special occasions.

After arrival in Lisbon, I had made official calls on senior officers of the three Portuguese Armed Services, but after that I dealt on a working basis with Brigadier Alfredo Delesque Sintra, chief of the Air Force, or with his second-in-command, who was Colonel Craveiro Lopes, later President of Portugal. The Brigadier had a sparkling personality, but the Colonel was of a rather dour demeanour though pleasant enough to deal with. I also became friendly with officers of the Portuguese Naval Air Service, who once took me up for a flight round the bay in one of their small twin-engined amphibians, an outing that almost ended in disaster when the brakes failed after we got back on the ground.

Another person I saw regularly was Colonel Humberto Delgado, who was in charge of the newly-formed Department of Civil Aviation. He was a smallish, thickset man, whose few remaining hairs were well-oiled and brushed lovingly round the side of his otherwise bald head. He was a very volatile personality, always bubbling over with excited conversation, wisecracks and laughter. His antics sometimes bordered on clownishness, and often it was difficult to take him seriously. He was not the kind of person who made people afraid, and it therefore came as a surprise to me to hear the news that, many years after the war, he supposedly came to a sticky end for political reasons somewhere near the Portuguese/Spanish frontier. He never gave me the impression of being especially ambitious and, certainly in those days, he did not seem to be cut out for the role of a political conspirator.

I was friendly with Colonel Delgado's number two, Captain Antonio Quintino da Costa, who taught me fencing. We used to drive twice a week to a huge Physical Health Institute on the outskirts of Lisbon, where he put me through the hoop.

'Hold your foil like a little bird; strongly enough for it not to escape, but gently enough not to hurt it!' he used to cry.

He knew exactly when to declare a minute's rest, just at the moment when I was ready to burst from exertion. The exercise was beneficial and served to cancel out the inroads made by the large quantities of port wine we drank in those days.

The first time we went to the Physical Health Institute, I noticed dark brown patches beside the fencing strip and asked the Captain what they were.

'Oh, blood,' he replied airily. 'Someone was killed here in a duel last week.'

From my understanding of his explanation, duels were then illegal in Portugal, but any Army officer who refused one was cashiered. Two Army officers, he said, had recently failed to kill each other in a duel over a matter of the heart and so one had been banished to the north and the other to the south of Portugal. They were said to be walking towards each other through Portugal, both armed with carbines.

Captain Quintino da Costa also told me about a famous duel that had been fought there not long previously between a patient and his doctor. The patient did not think the doctor had taken out his appendix efficiently and therefore challenged him. The doctor knew nothing at all about fencing, but his challenger was an expert with the sabre, the weapon chosen for their duel.

During the few minutes before the duel began, the patient took hold of his sabre in a professional manner and flexed his muscles gracefully, while the doctor grabbed his own weapon and had to be restrained by his seconds from advancing precipitately upon his opponent. When commanded to begin the fight, the patient adopted an expert fencing position en garde, whereupon the doctor, who made up for in courage what he lacked in experience, grabbed his opponent's sabre in his left hand – which was cut badly – and brought his own weapon down on top of his patient's head, thereby ending the contest. The ironic part of the affair was that the doctor spent the rest of the day putting stitches in his patient's head.

There was an unfortunate incident when our youthful Military Attaché made a courtesy call on a rather aged Portuguese general. During their conversation, the general remarked, 'My dear sir, you are very young to be a brigadier', to which our MA replied, 'My dear sir, you are very old to be a general.' This was apparently said in humorous vein, but it was not the sort of stuff to cement Anglo/Portuguese relations. We eventually persuaded a reluctant MA that he must write a letter of apology to the general concerned. He drafted something, but made the mistake of ending up with a double negative, a course that can often prove dangerous. In this case, he chose to use the word '*senão*', which in this particular context could be translated as 'anything but'. He intended to end his letter to the general with a flourish by saying, 'I do not wish for anything but good relations with you, my general, and with all other members of the Portuguese general staff.' In his final version of the letter, he unfortunately left out the 'anything but', with the result that his letter said he did not wish for good relations with the general and all other members of the Portuguese general staff. After that, the MA could not really sit down and write yet another letter of apology to the general and so he left the matter there. The Portuguese must have thought he was halfway round the bend, since their own dealings with diplomats and diplomatic matters were extremely punctilious and correct.

I well recall a luncheon given on 7 June 1945 at a fort near Estoril by the Minister of War for our MA, just before his transfer back to the UK. He was convinced that the Portuguese were going to give him the Order of Aviz and asked me to help him prepare a speech in advance to be used on the day of the luncheon to thank the Minister for the decoration. I remonstrated with him and said it was most unlikely the Portuguese would give him a gong, since we British could not normally receive such honours without permission being sought in advance. Nevertheless, he pressed on with the preparation of his speech, saying to me that after all the American MA had recently been given this gong.

The day of the luncheon was very hot, but the temperature inside the thick-walled fort near Estoril was agreeably cool. After a good meal, we repaired to a kind of office or study, where there was a large writing desk. Our eyes were immediately drawn to a parcel sitting on top of the desk, which was clearly the MA's farewell present. It looked awfully big to be a container of the Order of Aviz, but we thought perhaps there was a lot of packing material round it for protection. The Minister of War made a speech thanking the MA for his services and, at the end of it, presented him with the parcel, not even mentioning the Order of Aviz. As the MA unwrapped the parcel, we all watched in the way that children do when waiting for a conjuror to produce a rabbit out of a hat.

The poor MA's face was a picture when he finally found himself holding a heavily-wrought Portuguese silver inkpot. Poor chap, it could not have been easy for him to alter his speech of thanks to cope with the situation nor to hide his disappointment at not receiving the hallowed Order of Aviz.

I once had my own problems about Portuguese decorations when telling an aide to the Portuguese President about an official banquet my wife and I had attended where everyone was in full evening dress and simply dripping with scrambled egg, the term we used in the RAF for gold braid and decorations. I told the aide that the Portuguese present had been impressively turned out in their orders and decorations and that one of the most eye-catching of them was a wide purple ribbon or sash worn across the boiled shirts of its honoured owner.

'My dear fellow', he said. 'That is the Order of Christ and of course you shall have it.'

'No, no', I replied, 'that is not what I meant at all. I just wanted to say how impressive it looked.'

'Yes, of course', he replied. 'It really is very nice and there is no need for you to be modest. I shall arrange for you to receive it as soon as possible.'

The more I fought to reject this honour, the more convinced he became that I was motivated by feelings of modesty and really wanted the Order. I told him that British officials could not normally receive foreign honours without permission to accept them first being sought in high quarters, adding that such permission was rarely ever granted. He remained adamant, until I finally played my trump card, which was to say that the Order of Christ was a Roman Catholic order and that it would therefore be difficult to confer it on me, a member of the Church of England. This argument served to choke him off, and I heard no more about it.

My opposite number in the American Embassy was Lieutenant Colonel Russell A. Cone, a nice chap from Champagne, Illinois, and his assistant Air Attaché was a Captain. Russ Cone was a thoroughly nice guy but clearly very suspicious of the British, like many Middle Westerners who had isolationist tendencies at about that time. He was always talking about the Limeys this and the Limeys that, until one day, when we had already became friends, I asked him what his conception of a Limey was.

'Well, Wimpy', he replied laughingly, 'my conception of a Limey is a guy in a top hat and a monocle and he's always pulling a fast one.'

I used to pull his leg about Middle Westerners, and eventually we got on like a house on fire.

His Captain assistant once brought the house down at one of the regular meetings we Service Attachés held with our American counterparts to swap information about recent events. He told us about a Liberator aircraft that had crashed and said that, on impact with the ground, the control column had cut the pilot's head off.

'Good Heavens', said somebody. 'You mean he was decapitated?'

'No, no', replied the Captain who had obviously not heard the question properly. 'He was the second pilot.'

We could not help laughing at this misunderstanding, even though the matter was so grisly.

I was once invited to a shoot at a country estate in the neighbourhood of Gavião, which was near the frontier with Spain. We left Lisbon by car and arrived there in the late evening after a drive of several hours. Next day, we came downstairs at about five o'clock in the morning hoping there would be a good breakfast to sustain us during what would probably prove to be a hard day. Alas, the meal consisted of a long succession of biscuits, cakes and sticky buns, without any tea or coffee to drink. I had finally decided to tuck into the cake for lack of anything better, when suddenly ham and eggs and coffee appeared. It was really a most remarkable meal.

The whole business was quite a bit different from the procedure employed on Scottish moors. I was led off through the undergrowth by one of our hosts in search of birds to shoot, and it was not long before he became disgruntled by the lack of action.

'It's no good', he said to me. 'It's too cold a day and the birds are getting up. You must come back on a warmer day when they are less active and then we can get them on the ground.'

Many hares were slaughtered and a few partridges got the chop as well. Fairly early on in the day, someone shot a fox, and I learned that this was the done thing at Portuguese shoots and considered to be quite an honour for the gun concerned. At the end of the day, we posed in a group beside the bag for a photograph, and some well-wisher, no doubt wishing to do me honour, kept placing that wretched fox at my feet. I kept pushing it away again and succeeded in getting it well away from me for the photograph.

Inevitably, some RAF aircraft crashed or crash-landed in Portugal during the war and, in such cases, any survivors were interned by the Portuguese authorities at Caldas da Rainha, a town about 100 kilometres north of Lisbon. They lived there under reasonable conditions in a hotel, but their movements were restricted.

One day, I received word that a RAF Beaufighter aircraft had crashed off the southern coast of Portugal, and I immediately took steps to find out what had happened to the crew of two. I dashed off by car to Caldas da Rainha as soon as word was received that the crew members had arrived there in the hotel. There was a terrific sing-song going on in the sitting room of the hotel, with the pilot of the Beaufighter banging out old favourites on the piano, while friendly Portuguese sat around trying to join in the songs. The booze flowed unceasingly and altogether we had a great party. Suddenly I was called to the telephone and was told that the local chief of police wished to speak to me.

'I know you are there at the hotel with the RAF aircrew', he said, 'and I want to tell you that you may take them away.'

This was unheard of, since up till now any such aircrew had been required to remain in Caldas da Rainha. Thinking that it might be some practical joke, I telephoned back to the chief of police and asked him whether he had rung me. He confirmed a bit testily that he had indeed just telephoned me and assured me that I was free to take the Beaufighter crew off to Lisbon.

At the end of a good party I put the two Beaufighter crew members in my car and we drove back to Lisbon, where they stayed with us for several days. They were a great pair and one of them, who played the banjo, kept us entertained with songs he accompanied on my guitar. In conversation one day I bemoaned the fact that English sausages, Wall's for example, were unobtainable in Portugal and, incredibly enough, it turned out that one of the crew members, the navigator I think, had some family connection with the Wall's sausage business in England.

I arranged for their repatriation by a roundabout route and altogether we were rather sorry to have such an amusing pair leave us. Many months after the end of the war, the RAF delivered some Beaufighter aircraft to the Portuguese Air Force and I went out to Portela airport to meet them when they were flown in. One of the first crews to get out of the aircraft proved to be our old Beaufighter pair who had stayed with us. They were in cracking form and one of them, bless him, was carrying a packet of Wall's sausages as a present for us.

Altogether, 1945 was a busy year. In March we received a visit from Air Vice-Marshal Geoffrey Bromet, SBO (Senior British Officer), Azores. A British Overseas Airways Corporation mission led by Sir William Welsh came to Lisbon, and I travelled with them on a short visit to Lagens, Azores. The great moment, of course, was Victory in Europe Day on May 8, when huge crowds of flag-waving Portuguese thronged the street in front of the British Embassy, hundreds of them giving the victory sign. After church service that evening, members of the British community were invited to the Embassy residence, where the Ambassador gave an address.

I missed this part of the fun because I had been summoned to London several days previously for consultations and in fact spent the night of VE Day flying back to Lisbon. The thought that the war in Europe was over produced a warm glow, and I had a celebratory drink at the Sandbanks Hotel before catching the DC3.

The Allies took over the Axis diplomatic representations' premises in Lisbon, and it was my job to go together with Russ Cone and take over the offices of Colonel Hashagen, the German Air Attaché. I remarked semi-jokingly to Russ that many of the Nazis were a fanatical lot and expressed the hope that Hashagen would not make any last-ditch effort to bump us off. Russ and I arranged to meet half an hour before the takeover at a small establishment called the Vic Bar, which was right across the street from the entrance to the British Embassy. It was a pleasant little place, and many members of our Embassy had cultivated the habit of nipping across there for a quick one.

I met Russ as arranged in the bar at the appointed time and found that he had his Captain Assistant Air Attaché with him. After a couple of Martinis, I said it was time to leave for our meeting with Hashagen, whereupon Russ's assistant produced an enormous .45 automatic pistol from his inside breast pocket.

'Don't worry, Wimpy', said Russ. 'If that guy Hashagen makes any move, then my assistant here will drill him.'

I impressed upon Russ that we were going to take over a defeated enemy and that we must therefore not shake hands with Hashagen or fraternize in any way. The object of the exercise, I said, was merely to get Hashagen to hand over his office to us and give us the combinations of any safes that might be in it. We realized there would not be any interesting documents still around, as the Germans had spent several days before VE Day burning papers in the garden of their Embassy Residence.

Russ and I waited on a sofa in the front hall of the German Attachés' offices until Hashagen finally arrived, twenty minutes after the appointed time. Perhaps overcome by the excitement of the moment, Russ sprang forward, shook him warmly by the hand and said, 'Hello, Hashagen, how are you?'

I was very annoyed and remained scowling in the background during this exchange.

Enormous quantities of food were provided at luncheon and dinner parties in Portugal in those days, a far cry from the meagre rations of wartime England. For example, my wife and I attended a banquet given by the Portuguese Minister of Foreign Affairs at the Palacio das Necessidades on 29 June 1945, when we ate our way through a six-course dinner consisting of soup, salmon, asparagus, pheasant, ice cream and fruit. This was washed down with Madeira Sercial 1897, Buçaco white wine 1918, Curia rosé 1930, Buçaco red wine 1920, Super-Reserve champagne, Offley port and liqueurs. I don't think I could eat even half that amount nowadays at one sitting.

One had to be in good training, as I found when making an official visit to Oporto in the following month. One of my principal hosts was Geoffrey Tait, who was then President of the British Legion there and a descendant of one of the long-established British families in Oporto. Another was a nice man called Cecil Pheysey. They took me for lunch to the famous Factory House, an old building which was the headquarters of about sixteen British port wine-shipping firms. I had heard about this place being hallowed ground so far as port was concerned and wondered desperately whether I should have to go a couple of hours without a cigarette. Not a bit of it, we went into a small bar, sherry was served, and many people lit up cigarettes.

I was shown the ballroom, which had been kept exactly as it was at the moment when victory at the Battle of Waterloo had been announced.

Then we went in to lunch in the famous dining room, of which there are two identical ones; one ate in the first and then moved in to the second at the end of the meal in order that the odour of food should not spoil the taste of port wine. It was quite a hot day and the port fairly flew round the table, a decanter of tawny being closely pursued by one of vintage. Flunkeys passed bowls of ice, and I imitated my companions by placing a cube in my glass of port. I remarked to my neighbour that such use of ice in the home of port had come as a great surprise to me since I should previously have considered the practice to border on heresy. He replied that in warm weather it was accepted practice to place an ice cube in one's glass of port and leave it there for up to a maximum of thirty seconds before removing it. If left longer than that, he said, the port would go sick and be unsuitable for drinking.

I glanced across the table at Stanley Yeatman, one of the stalwarts of Oporto wine shipping, who had the reputation of drinking one bottle of vintage port a day, and decided that my capacity was puny by comparison. After lunch, I had to go for a two-hour drive to blow the fumes out of my head before continuing with official calls.

On 22 August 1945, there was a bullfight in Algés which was billed as a 'great *corrida* in honour of the victory of the United Nations in the presence of HE the President of the Republic and the Diplomatic Corps, eight wild and powerful bulls from the famous ranch of Palha Blanco'. I missed this event because the Air Ministry had summoned me back to London to act as escorting officer to the Brazilian Air Minister, Joaquim Salgado Filho, who was making an official visit to the UK with his wife and several officers of the Brazilian Air Force.

The visit was pretty hectic, and all the running around on official calls plus the extensive wining and dining nearly drove me up the wall. One pleasant interlude during the visit was when we took the Minister, who was also President of the Brazilian Jockey Club at that time, to York races and saw the St Leger run on 5 September and won by Squadron-Leader Stanhope Joel's Chamossaire in good style.

Our next excitement was the negotiation and signing of the Anglo-Portuguese Civil Aviation Agreements in Lisbon during the early part of December 1945. Our mission was led, if I remember rightly, by Ivor

Thomas, Parliamentary Under-Secretary for Air, and that of the Portuguese by Marcello Mathias. Our two main negotiating officials on the mission were Cribbet and Cheetham, a formidable-sounding combination of names.

I was about to leave the members of our mission at the front entrance of the Portuguese Ministry for Foreign Affairs, when John Cheetham, who was from the Foreign Office, asked me whether any of the Portuguese negotiators spoke English.

'I don't believe that any of them do', was my reply.

'In that case, you had better come in and be our interpreter', he said.

Phew, what a job! The whole negotiation went through like a dose of salts, and in the process of translating back and forth I learned a great deal about the Fifth Freedom and other facets of civil aviation agreements. After the signing, the Portuguese gave us a nice celebratory dinner in Estoril at which some excellent wines were served, including an 1835 Bual Madeira and an 1863 Borges port.

In early 1946, I conceived the idea of getting a RAF football team to come and play a match against the Portuguese in Lisbon, half the proceeds to go to the RAF Benevolent Fund. It required a tremendous amount of organization, especially so far as publicity was concerned, but fortunately we had an excellent Press Attaché called Horace Zino, who coped admirably. We had to face problems of every kind. For example, a Portuguese wine producer sent me cases of sparkling wine labelled 'RAF Grand Vin Mousseux', with a RAF roundel on the label. I reported this to the Air Ministry, which took an extremely dim view and made me send back all the wine and prohibit the producer from using 'RAF' or the roundel on the label.

Our team arrived in Lisbon by air on 16 February 1946 and it looked rather like an all-England line-up consisting of: Williams, Scott, Barker, Soo, Franklin, Paterson, Dougall, Brown, Matthews (the immortal Stanley), Fenton and Smith. Their opponents, billed as a Group of the Portuguese Army, looked rather like a Portuguese national team.

The match was played on 17 February in the National Stadium and ended in a 1-1 draw, a diplomatic result welcomed by myself, even though our men had been expected to wallop the locals. The stadium was packed and the game was played in the presence of the President of Portugal. The Portuguese provided a splendid banquet in Estoril, after which Brigadier

Sintra presented mementoes to the English players, and an RAF officer, Air Vice-Marshal Paterson I think, did the same for the Portuguese. I had been through many harrowing experiences during the organization of this match, but suddenly it all became worthwhile when I found myself able to send a cheque for £3,000, our share of the proceeds, to the RAF Benevolent Fund.

Our last excitement before transfer back to the UK was the visit of HMS *Nelson* to Lisbon from 22 to 28 March 1946 on her way home to be broken up. She was escorted by about seven destroyers, whose captains and officers were extremely hospitable. 'Drop in for a pink gin around noon', was their daily invitation. The trouble was that these destroyers were tied up one outside the other and it always seemed that the one you were invited to was the outside of the seven. This meant that one was invited for a drink in every destroyer on the way to the outside one, and very often on the way back as well.

Naturally, there was a lot of official entertainment, since this was an official visit. There was a reception at the British Embassy on 23 March and two days later a gala performance at the São Carlos Theatre by the National Symphonic Orchestra with the incomparable Guilhermina Suggia as soloist. I think it was at the ball afterwards that one of the British Captains came out with a classic remark. He was dancing with a very pretty Portuguese girl, who pointed out a distinguished-looking man and said, 'That's my husband. He is the Minister of Economic Affairs.'

'Oh', replied our gallant Captain off the cuff: 'Can we have an economic affair?' This amused the lady no end, and apparently also her husband, when she told him about it.

The Portuguese gave a party for the ratings in the local zoological garden which turned out to be something of a chaotic affair. Signs were put up saying, 'This way to the white wine', 'This way to the red wine', 'This way to the brandy', and the thirsty ratings needed no urging to follow them, especially as it was rather a warm day. The situation eventually became altogether too cheerful, and I was told that one of the ratings was found joyously sharing a bath with the hippopotami. Thank Heavens, there were no accidents or serious incidents.

The President and Madame Carmona gave a super banquet for the Fleet at the Ajuda Palace (which had been specially opened for the affair) on 26 March , and the visit was rounded off next day when the Commander-in-Chief, Captains and Officers of the British Fleet invited us to a reception on board HMS *Nelson*. We felt sad when we later saw the old ship sailing away down the Tagus on her last journey home, but were at least glad that the week's official visit to Lisbon had been a pretty good swansong for her. And most of us felt that our constitutions badly needed a rest after a week of such lavish hospitality, pink gin by now practically coming out of our ears. It was also our own swansong, since my wife and I had exactly one more month to go in Lisbon before being posted back to the UK for demobilization.

Chapter 12

Finale

We returned to the UK on 28 April 1946 expecting that I should be demobilized within a short space of time and then sent back with my family to Brazil at public expense as a returning volunteer. It turned out to be not quite as simple as that.

Many of us in those days had been amused by a joke – I think it was by David Langdon in *Punch* magazine – showing an RAF medical officer, who had carried out a routine medical examination of a candidate for demobilization, saying, 'I am very sorry, Flight Lieutenant, but you are unfit to leave the Royal Air Force.' I thought this very funny until precisely the same thing happened to me. The medico said I was unfit to leave the Service because of my bad ear and made me undergo three weeks of treatment. At the end of it, I was pronounced well enough to leave and was duly demobilized on 22 May 1946.

Many people found it strange to be fitted out with civvy hats and coats on demobilization, after having worn uniform for so many years. We tried on our new acquisitions and eyed ourselves dubiously in long mirrors provided in the fitting-out stores. The suits were not exactly Savile Row cut and the hats were a bit odd. Nevertheless, I think it was a very good show on the part of the government to equip us with these items on return to civvy street. I was granted 116 days release leave ending on 15 September 1946 and was given some princely sum like £130 as my final pay-off. On the strength of it we rented a flat in Halkin Place, off Belgrave Square, which was nice but really a bit too expensive for us. Still, we were young and relatively carefree in those days and suffering from some immediate post-war headiness. I had received a tip that The Bug had a good chance of winning the Wokingham Stakes and put a fiver on him when he was still seven to one against. He duly won his race in fine style and the £35 I won came in handy for the rent, this sum being equivalent in those days to about half a month's pay for a Wing Commander.

I received a nice letter from the Air Ministry dated 27 August 1946 which said:

> Sir,
>
> Upon the occasion of your resigning your commission, I am commanded by the Air Council to convey to you their thanks for the services which you have rendered to the Royal Air Force during a period of grave national emergency.

The war was over, and all I wanted now was to return to my farm in Brazil with my wife, small son and Portuguese nanny we had acquired in Lisbon. The quickest way to get there was by the newly-formed British South American Airways, but for this priorities were necessary. One could only obtain places on flights by queuing up at a particular point in the Dorchester Hotel, and it was not easy at that time to get four places on the same aircraft. I stood for hours in the Dorchester and finally found myself at the head of the queue. Hooray, I thought, we're practically on our way at last. At that moment, the person attending to supplicants for priorities informed me that the aircraft was full and instructed me to return the following week for a booking.

We moved into a hotel, cursing the bad luck that had prevented us at the last moment from getting on to this flight. A couple of days later, some friends came round for a drink and I told them all about the queue at the Dorchester and how furious I was that we had been pipped at the post.

'But didn't you know?' asked the husband of the couple. 'That aircraft crashed at Bathurst and everybody on board was killed.'

My good luck had held once again.

Appendix I

Article from *Cosmopolitan* magazine, 1943

WE LIGHT THE TARGET
By Squadron Leader
RICHARD ANTHONY WELLINGTON, D.S.O., D.F.C.
With BOB CONSIDINE
INS Foreign Correspondent

We asked the British for an all-clear on the hush-hush subject of Pathfinder pilots. They said 'Yes', and here is the first inside story on those daring pilots and crews, as related by one of them.

This was my sixtieth – and perhaps final – bombing mission. When it was over, I would have a real egg (the old-fashioned kind with a shell around it) waiting for me. Plus a goodly share of the fifty pints of beer our chaps had accumulated and tenderly put away against the time when we could celebrate the completion of our long operational span.

I was as scared as I was on my first mission, back in the timeless reaches of 1940. But that was all right. I didn't have the bad feeling: the feeling a chap seems to get when he knows he's not coming back. I was just scared, as usual, and I knew that would make me a little keener up there, a little more wide-awake.

It was to be a big show. Düsseldorf. There would be perhaps a thousand bombers, many of them Lancasters. We never talk much about the number of bombers involved in a mission. But we knew that this night would see an all-out effort, because many Pathfinders were going to be on the raid.

The Pathfinder has been on the hush-hush list since the inception of a curious brand of trail-blazing more than a year ago. Only now are we permitted to speak even in general terms about our work. There are still many things about a Pathfinder bomber which cannot be revealed, but we can talk about the Pathfinders themselves, the blokes who find distant targets in the dead of night, light them up with fire bombs and flares, and make possible the indescribable precision of the countless bombers which follow us.

I am a Pathfinder pilot, and have been since January, 1943. Before that I had flown for nine months for Wing Commander Guy Gibson, V.C., who led the fabulous raids on the Mohne and Eder dams. I went to him, after reading the bulletin board's call for volunteers for the then mysterious business named Pathfinding, and told him that my chaps and I would like to have a crack at such work. I understood vaguely that the RAF was to train a group of fliers to mark the targets for the main bulk of Bomber Command's aircraft, and that we were giving up the old practice of having the first few bombers over the target drop a host of incendiaries to aid the main force which followed.

'They need good crews in this work,' Gibson told me. Then he added jovially (I believe), 'And I doubt if you'll get in.'

There was need above everything else, I was told, for experienced operational crews to lead the way to the target, 'mark' it for the rest of the Bomber Command, which was now quickly expanding with many new crews. Now, you know, of course, that when bombers set off for a target deep inside Germany, each has to find its way there on its own, pin-point its landmarks, make sure it is over the target, and drop its bombs on the aiming point. Given good navigation, the whole business sounds simple. But navigation at night is not as simple as that, when the winds vary from those the meteorological pundits have given, landmarks like rivers have five or six similar bends, and cumulus clouds must be circled. Then, too, the target itself is surrounded by searchlights which blot out ground detail and bedazzle pilot and bombardier. In addition, around the target, one finds smoke screens and decoys.

For the Jerries are great on decoys. Dummy incendiaries glow, false factories blaze toward heaven with their skeleton roofs and red windows outlined against red flames. In addition, these decoys are judiciously located never too far away from the targets, often with some duplicate landmark to lend greater weight to their lie. The RAF knew that only exceptional pilots or the most experienced operational crews could be certain of sorting out the true aiming point from the false. And now such crews were needed to form a Pathfinder Force. These crews would be the first on the scene, with their specialist navigators and pilots. The decoys would not distract them from their expert intensive target identification. Having made quite sure, they would drop their colored flares and markers. If the weather was clear, these markers would burn on the aiming point, I was told, and if it was cloudy, the flares would hang precisely over the target, drawing the devastating might of the Bomber Command.

So I joined the Pathfinders.

Up to that point, I had been on thirty-four missions, but I had to take a host of examinations, physical and mental, before I could qualify. I had to prove that I could identify at least fifteen stars; that I knew as much about my aircraft as the men who built it; that I was more than an amateur at meteorology; that my crew had confidence in me and I in them.

After six operational flights we were given the golden eagle badge which Pathfinders wear. Tonight, on my sixtieth mission (and my twenty-sixth as a Pathfinder) I would win permanent possession of that badge. It is not awarded permanently until the completion of one's operational span, except in the case of a Pathfinder killed in action. In such cases he is awarded the badge permanently and posthumously.

The preparations for the final mission were as familiar as a tense and oft-repeated dream. It was at ten o'clock in the morning that we learned that just about every available Pathfinder would be on the operation.

There were the usual things to do, and the first of these was testing our aircraft on a thirty-minute flight. There was luncheon – absent-mindedly eaten – and then, at four o'clock, the briefing. There we learned that the target was Düsseldorf. We were lectured on the last-known defences of that city; instructed about its population and its more vital factories; told what kind of weather we could expect; shown many maps and mosaics of our targets and told – as usual – how important it was to destroy these things. I thought for a moment about the death and destruction we would be the harbinger of, but one soon loses such emotions. You think only that you're on a big, spectacular show, and that you'd ten times rather be a part of it than not.

When the long briefing was over, I went back to our mess to wait. That's always the hardest part. Someone turned on the radio, but few listened to it. Some wrote letters. Some of us picked up newspapers (and a few of us held them upside down, until a chap with more ice water in his veins politely turned them around). The usual jokers sprang the usual jokes. For instance, we're given a real egg and bacon before the mission, and get the same delicacy after we get back. So a familiar joke was for a bloke to approach another and say, 'If you don't come back tonight, can I have your egg?'

Five o'clock now – and that egg and bacon. And the vitamin and halibut-oil pills, for vision's sake, and the interminable wait – broken once by a chap who paraphrased the Prime Minister's famous line by saying: 'Never in the history of the world have so many done so little for so long.'

But at last it was time to dress. I put on my heaviest underwear, my battle dress, two sweaters, two pairs of heavy socks and the fleece-lined boots. And emptied all my pockets – the precaution we take in case of capture.

We stopped by the crew room, where the gunners (who are more exposed to the extreme cold) put on electrically heated suits. All of us tested our helmets, to be sure built-in phones were working. We were handed a can of orange juice, a bar of chocolate, a stick of chewing gum and one or two other things about which I'm not permitted to write.

It is getting dark now as we go to our aircraft, climb in, talk things over with the ground crew and start the four Merlin engines. Their sound is comforting. We taxi slowly down the perimeter track, our navigation lights blinking on, and at long, long last – and on the precise scheduled minute – we rumble down the black runway and take off.

They know we're coming, of course. But your thoughts go to other things: stern Pathfinding tasks such as setting a true course, making certain that the ever-changing wind is reckoned with, making absolutely certain up there in the impenetrable gloom that we lead our bombers exactly to the right place.

We're on our own now, as we head out over the Channel. There is no such thing as formation flying at night. We go along in what amounts to single file and except on bright moonlit nights – and this night of the Düsseldorf mission was not one – we see no other friendly planes.

My navigator, Tommy Blair, and my combination bomb-aimer and map-reader huddle over their dimly lighted maps. My flight engineer, sitting in the co-pilot's seat, attends to the job of the throttles and searches the skies. My gunners are on the alert, remembering the lessons taught them by their Wing-Commander, the RAF's great night-vision authority, who has proved there is no such thing as night blindness if a man is properly schooled in the use of his eyes in the dark. The gunners (and all of us) search the darkest corners of the black heavens, for enemy fighters lurk there.

Now we're coming toward the coast. My tail gunner, his fingers itchy on the triggers of his cluster of four machine guns, spots a night-fighter. I toss our big aircraft into an evasive action, and we get away. Now the searchlights on the coast begin reaching out for us. I recognize the lights, and that's comforting because it means we're on the right course. I turn the Lancaster's nose toward each light fanning our way. That seems to be the best way of avoiding them.

The target is hours away and the night presses in against us. Beneath us, now and then, the searchlights come on and hot hoses of ack-ack come up lazily, it seems, and then streak past us.

You sit there with the controls in your gloved hands, your eyes trying to pierce the night ahead of you, your ears alerted against any warning that might come over the aircraft's intercommunications system. You're ready to throw your aircraft into the most violent kind of evasive action if attacked – gyrations that, for some reason, a pilot would not dream of performing in the daylight.

But this long approach to the target which you must illuminate, so that perhaps a thousand other planes can eradicate it, is also a time for reflection. On this trip – my swan song if I am unlucky enough to be given a desk job or an instructor's rôle – my own background for war passed somewhere through my mind. I thought again how strange it was to be doing this at all, when only a short time before (as time is measured by the calendar) I had looked forward to a life on my cattle ranch near São Paulo, Brazil, where my father still operates a railroad.

I thought a little of Harrow, where I went to school, and wondered what had become of the chaps I knew there. I thought of my keen disappointment when I wasn't assigned to a Spitfire squadron.

I thought, too, of my missions. I was on the first 1,000–plane raid, back in pre-Pathfinder days, and the mushrooming brilliance of seeing 8,000 pound block–busters explode was still with me. Three times to Berlin (and a memory of my irrelevant hopes that my bombs didn't destroy my favorite Berlin night-club, the Shanghai) . . . Three times to Hamburg, the city which ran like lava . . . Essen, the night a piece of flak blew out the windshield in front of me, and I had no goggles. It was 45 below and I thought my eyeballs had frozen . . . Twice to Cologne, wondering about the Cathedral . . . Genoa, where we arrive a full minute late, and the Italians trained their searchlights on the water instead of the air (and later trained them on the air when a pal of mine was raising hell on the water in a motor torpedo boat)) . . . Mannheim . . . Karlsruhe . . . Dortmund . . . Duisberg . . . the countless times over the Ruhr, when they threw everything at us.

There were thoughts, too, of pals who are gone now. And of their deaths: the red debris of their collisions, the direct hits by ack-ack and the great red ball of flame they made when their bombs and their petrol tanks exploded in the air, and the strange way in which their tiny incendiaries went sputtering down through the night, and the ugly black cloud that we flew through – which was all that was left of them.

I thought of one of the Hamburg missions, when we smelled the flak. You can smell it, sharp and acrid and frightening. Frightening because you don't smell it until it is too close. The flak going through one of my wings and setting a petrol tank on fire, making us the cynosure of all eyes below. The flak that burst through the window of my compartment and lodged in the neck of my flight engineer, Tash Goodwin, and dug into the spine of my bomb-aimer, Johnny Cunningham, and blew away part of the hand of my wireless operator, little Tich Webster. It hit us on our bomb run, when we couldn't take evasive action, but we stuck there – committed to the course – and Cunningham, though he was very weak, remained at his post. And then when it was time to open the bomb-bay doors, they were jammed – and we had to take our great load all the way back home, with the wing burning and one engine gone. I counted 278 holes in our aircraft when I got it home, and then stopped counting.

But now there was Düsseldorf to think about. The weather was turning bad, but we knew our navigator would lead us right to it. We droned along, snaking this way and that when the lights reached out for our aircraft. The fighters were getting thicker now, and I thought of the time when a Focke-Wulf loomed up only a few yards ahead of me, going at a terrific clip, and how our Lancaster lurched upward to avert the head-on collision.

The gunners are now on the triple alert whenever the ack-ack slackens. That usually means that Jerry fighters are moving up on us. Now it happens again, as it has happened before, and I can hear the angry rattle of our guns and I fling the big aircraft into an 80-degree bank. The tracer goes safely past us.

The lights are thicker now, as we come closer to Düsseldorf. They must not cone us. I had seen more than one of our aircraft coned brightly and blown to bits in a few seconds. And I had been coned. Time and space and speed lose all significance when you are pin-pointed by a great cone of lights. Your brain reels and you think in slow motion. You appear to be fastened on those lights as securely as a butterfly is pinned against the plush background of a museum case. You squirm and you hurl your aircraft about, while the stuff comes up at you, and when you pray and pry yourself loose (if you do) you are short of breath.

But Düsseldorf . . . Indelibly our targets present themselves in my mind. We must light them as if they were bathed in pitiless sunlight. We must light them exactly on time, for the bombers carrying high explosives and incendiaries are behind us, depending on us to lead them to the correct place, at the correct time.

There – ahead. 'Steady . . . steady', Cunningham's voice sounds in the earphones. Below us and now behind us a factory blazes brightly, a little lake shines. But when you've been a Pathfinder long enough you can spot the frauds, and these are frauds – cleverly built by Jerry to trap us into dropping our bombs here. Jerry's decoy factories always burn *too* brightly. Besides, we have other ways of finding the real ones.

High over us the Jerry fighters drop their inevitable flare path, slow-falling flares that form an avenue down which we must fly, in a straight path, to get where he knows we want to get. It is a path bright as Piccadilly will be, one of these nights. But down it we go.

'Left . . . Left. Steady. Right!' Cunningham says.

'Right!' I repeat.

'Bomb doors open,' Cunningham requests quietly, while we fly through the black balloons of Jerry's heavy ack-ack.

'Bomb doors open', I say.

'Coming up . . . coming up . . . almost up . . . and then a deep well of silence in the middle of the infernal boom of the engines and the bark of the ack-ack. It is broken, as always, by Cunningham's voice, still quiet but with a new note in it.

'Bombs gone!'

'Okay. Bombs gone. Bomb door closed.'

And now the Lancaster is like a raging bronco, released from strong fetters. I hang it up on its props, dive it, bank it and slither away from the terrible lights. We sweep wide on the prearranged get-away course, and now we can see our targets – tremendously alight. Not only from our heavy fire bombs, which defy extinguishing, but from our parachute flares and our incendiaries' work about the ruins caused by high-explosive bombs.

There is more talk on the intercom now; talk of what the subsequent bombers will do to targets so plainly visible. Bomber Command sent over 2,000 tons of bombs to Düsseldorf that night. Five times as many as destroyed our Coventry. We tell each other over the intercom to stay alert; that they'll fight us all the back to the Channel.

There was our field at last, with its phosphorus-like landing area, the welcome signal to come in, and a feeling – when the ship had stopped rolling – that is beyond my descriptive powers. All I can say is that there is no emotion that can parallel the sensation of knowing you've found your target, ignited it for the others to see, and are home safely.

There was the real egg and the bacon to eat, and the fifty pints to share. Our chaps opened the bar at six in the morning. I got plastered.

Appendix II

Targets – Operations

1942	**RAW based at 106 Squadron, A Flight, RAF Coningsby**

30 May   Operations Cologne, 1.000 raid.

01 June   Operations Essen, 1.000 raid.
25 June   Operations Bremen, landed Woodhall, 1.000 raid.
29 June   Operations Bremen. 8 SBC.

26 July   Operations Hamburg. 14 SBC's (aircraft hit by flak, 3 of crew wounded, tyre burst, brought bombs back, fired at enemy fighter).
30 July   Operations Düsseldorf. Good prang.

06 August   Operations Duisburg. 10 SBCs, cloud.
08 August   Gardening Skagerrak. 5 Veg, Anholt Island. Very bad weather.
11 August   Operations Mainz. 10 SBC's. Photos taken. Good prang.
12 August   Operations Mainz. 12 SBC's. 4 flares.
15 August   Operations Düsseldorf. 10 SBC's, 3 flares, cloud.
16 August   Gardening Salzniz. Dropped veg (5) safe in North Sea.
24 August   Operations Frankfurt. 12 SBC's. Cloud over target. 16 Bundles Nickels.
27 August   Operations Cassel. Recco' of target.

01 September   Operations Saarbrücken. 12 SBC's.
10 September   Operations Düsseldorf. 12 SBC's. Outer STB engine cut over Dutch coast. Returned and jettisoned bombs in sea.

13 September	Operations Bremen – 12 SBC's. Port outer airscrew chipped by flak.
14 September	Operations Wilhelmshaven. 12 SBC's. Turned back on receiving SYKO message. Brought all bombs back.
16 September	Operations Essen. 12 SBC's. Flak very heavy and accurate. A/C hit, Outer SBD engine hit. Bit rev. levers. Shaken rigid.
19 September	Operations Munich. 6 SBC's. Nickels.
23 September	Operations Wismar, unable to locate target due to cloud. Bad weather. Bombs released on Lübeck.

01 October   RAW based at 106 Squadron, RAF Syerston

01 October	Operations Wismar. 14 SBC's. Hydraulics U/S. Bomb doors open. Pulled bottle. Diverted Leconfield.
05 October	Operations Aachen. 12 SBC's, hazy.
06 October	Operations Osnabruck. 14 SBC's.
17 October	Daylight Operations. Le Creusot. 14 SBC's.
22 October	Operations Genoa (Italy). Photo 1½ miles Aiming point. Landed Tempsford.
24 October	Daylight Operations Milan (Italy). Returned. Lack of cloud cover. Brought bombs back.

RAW grounded for 2 months – sick leave

Total flying for 1942: 363.25 hours.

1943

03 January	Operations Essen. 10 SBC's. Special flares. 14 aircraft on target.
08 January	Operations Duisburg. 12 SBC's. Flak A/C hit. Feathered outer port engine. Returned three.
09 January	Operations Essen. 12 SBC's. Flak through windscreen.
11 January	Operations Essen. 12 SBC's. Jettisoned in sea. Starboard engine overheating on climb. Oxygen U/S. Hydraulics U/S. Blew bottle.

12 January	Operations Essen. 12 SBC's. Photo of aiming flares.
16 January	Berlin. Easy trip.
17 January	Operations Berlin. Flak much heavier. Photo of subs engine factory 3 miles SSW 1 Templehof.
30 January	Operations Hamburg. 12 SBC's. Bombed aiming flares. Landed Fulbeck.

February 1943   **RAW based at Pathfinder Force, B Flight, 83 Squadron, RAF Wyton**

13 February	Operations Lorient (France). Flares 14,000ft. Bomb 12,000 ft. Photo 310 o – 1 mile.
14 February	Operations Spezia (Italy). Flares. 4 AfC on target. Direct hit on AP.
16 February	Operations Lorient (France). TI's Markers.
19 February	Operations Wilhelmshaven. Markers. Cloud. Attacked by ME 109
21 February	Operations Bremen. 4 TI's. Cloud.
26 February	Operations Cologne. 4 TI's.
28 February	Operations Saint-Nazaire (France). 8 SBC and flares. Dropped bomb. Sight U/S. 5 holes. Coned in both searchlights. Shaky do!

01 March	Operations Berlin. 5 TI markers.
04 March	Operations Hamburg. 8 TI's.
05 March	Operations Essen
08 March	Operations Nuremberg. 2 TI green.
09 March	Operations Munich. 1 SBC flare. 2 TI green. 1 white Coned over target. Few holes.
11 March	Operations Stuttgart. 4 TI's green. Photo 3 miles AP.
12 March	Operations Essen. 4 TI green. 1 TI yellow.
22 March	Operations Saint-Nazaire (France). 4 TI red.
08 April	Operations Duisburg
10 April	Operations Frankfurt
13 April	Operations Spezia (Italy). Flares. Battleships not seen. Photo 1¼.

14 April	Operations Stuttgart. TI's green
16 April	Operations Pilsen (Czechoslovakia). 6 TI's. Flares. Hit by Karlsruhe flak.
26 April	Operations Duisburg. 6 TI's. Holed again.
04 May	Operations Dortmund. TI Reds. Fog on landing at base. Beam Landing (fine!).
12 May	Operations Duisburg. 4 TI's.
23 May	Operations Dortmund. 5 TI's. 2000 ton Prang.
29 May	Operations Wuppertal. 4 TI's.
11 June	Operations Düsseldorf. Good prang. Flak through Perspex. Last trip.

Operations:

Two tours or 60 sorties completed
+ 1 abortive: 2.30 hours.
Total operational hours: 334.15, all on Lancasters.
2 Daylights: 14.15 hours.
First sortie: 30 May 1942
Last sortie: 11 June 1943.

June 1943   RAW posted to 8 (PFF) HQ

Note:	RAF terms/Abbreviations
AP	= Aiming Point
AC/AfC	= Aicraft
Bottle	= Refers to the use of emergency hydraulic gear
Gardening	= Sowing mines in water from a low height
Nickels	= Airborne leaflet propaganda
SBC's	= Small bomb containers
TI's	= Target Indicators
U/S	= Unserviceable
Vegetables	= Magnetic mines

Pathfinder Pilot